AND, THE BIRDS

Danced

A Journey of
Hope
Through Paths of Pain and Grief

Debra Milleson White

Carpenter's Son Publishing

Published by Carpenter's Son Publishing, Franklin, Tennessee

Published in association with Larry Carpenter of Christian Book Services, LLC
www.christianbookservices.com

Edited by David Brown

Cover and Interior Layout Design by Suzanne Lawing

Printed in the United States of America

978-1-952025-72-3

To Roary Adam White ("Moe"), my love in heaven above, You are my heart honey and I thank God for choosing me to be your wife. I am forever grateful for the love you gave me and how you taught me to fully live each moment in life to the fullest!! Your amazing spirit lives forever in my heart and I will love you for a thousand years and beyond.

To my son, Jonathan, the first to give me the name of Mom! Thank you for listening to me during my tears and always being there for me. Thank you for making me smile and laugh when I need to smile and laugh the most. Your reminder to trust God is such a gift to my spirit! I love you and my daughter in law, Jessie. I am so proud of you both! I am beyond excited about meeting my first grandchild, my granddaughter this year!! Love, Mom

To my daughter, "El", I am so proud of your awareness of your true self and your honesty. Thank you for your help with technology, especially during my long hours of writing. Your insightfulness amazes me! I love you and my son in law, Matt and I am so proud of both of you!! Love, Mom

To my daughter, Abbey, I am so proud of the beautiful young woman you have become. Thank you for sharing your amazing gift for photography in this book. Thank you for teaching me how to slow down and capture all the moments around me! Your smile brightens my day! I am so proud of you and your accomplishments and I look forward to all that awaits as you enter college this year! I love your passion for diversity and inclusion!! Love, Mom

Contents

Introduction

Standing on Shifting Sand

She looked up with eyes reaching to look straight into her mommy's eyes. She spoke like she was much older than her years of four, and she boldly exclaimed, "Mommy, you have been all bound up, but you are about to be set free!" My daughter, at her young age, boldly announced this to me as if she could see the invisible chains wrapped tightly around me. Little did I know the journey that was ahead.

During the marriage I was in at the time to my first husband, Lyle , I had a strong sense of being unloved and unvalued. This added to the chains of untrue beliefs about myself that I was not worth even a crushed penny that had been stomped deeply into the pavement.

Although I had dreams of a fairytale love and tried to pretend Lyle and I lived in a great marriage, the truth is we were far from both.

As the years progressed during my marriage to Lyle, my heart was being chipped away one piece at a time as my sadness grew.

When my heart was sure something was not right with my marriage to Lyle, I would hear other wives talk about arguments with their husbands, and again tell myself, "See, no marriage is perfect. You are expecting too much." I lived in this cycle for years. Each time, my heart chipped away, breaking off more pieces.

What was I to do with those lingering broken pieces of my heart and pieces of shattered dreams of what I believed marriage should be? I guess there was no wonder I didn't know what love was; I didn't even love myself.

I had become very good at wearing the mask of pretending, and I began striving for perfection like I had when I was growing up. I was losing myself more and more. I took God out of the box I had kept him in and began praying more for God to help me, even though I didn't know what kind of help I needed.

My first marriage ended in divorce after eighteen years.

Yet another journey, unimaginable to my eyes and heart, was ahead of me. A journey that would reveal truth and value that I did not believe was inside of me.

Years later from my divorce, in my forties, I was standing on the shore of the beautiful blue ocean, just me and the birds on the shore. I felt my feet sinking into the sand deeper and deeper.

The ocean throughout the years has had a voice deeper than the sound of waves crashing or calmly swaying back and forth to me. It was at the ocean when God revealed to me a vision that began my journey of awareness, which we will unravel the layers of through this book.

I sat by the ocean, praying to God to help me understand my life and His ways. I also prayed for the desires of my heart. I had kept God in a "as needed box" for many of my years, and when I was young, I quickly learned to not talk about my problems.

Often through prayer, I feel God's presence while being outside in nature, in His creation. The beauty of His creation amazes me!

His love surrounds us! Whether during waves or sinking in shifting sand, the wind of the Holy Spirit carries us.

Years after my divorce, the desire in my heart for true love and a godly marriage grew stronger. During this time, I truly fell in love with Jesus and thought it would just be me and Jesus for life, just us. But God had a different plan! God restores!

Mutual friends introduced me to Moe, a caring and kind man who loved God and his family. Moe and I began dating, and during our years of dating, I found myself at times just watching him, fully taking in God's gift of this amazing man in my life.

I had a wall of protection around my heart for years that had to be chiseled away. I have heard that people who have been hurt deeply in the past sometimes sit back and watch when they are in new situations to make sure it is safe to get closer or interact. I saw that I waited and watched in all new situations as well.

Moe had so much love in his eyes and was so patient with me as I worked through breaking some lingering wall fragments that had protected my heart after experiencing past hurts that were deep inside me. Moe would sometimes say,

"Honey what is it going to take for you to know how much I truly love you?" He had so much patience with me, loving me right where I was. It was so nice to see love, kindness, and compassion and to be so in love!

We married years after dating, and I finally knew I was loved and I loved him so! My prayer for a godly, loving, compassionate, humble, and strong husband had been answered! God sent my husband, and we were so in love!

Zechariah 9:12 reads, "Return to your fortress, you prisoners of hope; even now I announce that I will restore twice as much to you." (NIV)[1]

Psalm 71:20 declares, "Though you have made me see troubles, many and bitter, you will restore my life again; from the depths of the earth you will again bring me up."[2]

Still newlyweds, my husband surprised me with a trip to the beach for Valentine's Day! We awoke, packed our suitcases, and traveled to the coast. We traveled as we normally did, holding one hand clenched together with the occasional gentle kiss to his hand I would give him. He would look at me and smile with those dimples making him even more handsome. My heart would melt! I thanked God every day for a love such as this He had given us.

We arrived at our room and unpacked and sat by the beautiful ocean that night.

The next morning, I awoke for a morning walk by the ocean.

Before I left that morning for my walk on the beach, I said to my husband, who was resting peacefully, "Honey, I am go-

1 NIV, See footnotes.
2 NIV, See footnotes.

ing to go walk by the beach and see the sunrise." I whispered, "I love you." He whispered back "I love you too, Honey."

I quietly opened the door of the oceanfront room on this Valentine's Day weekend and walked down the steps out onto the cool morning shifting sand. There was sand and water as far as I could see. I felt the cool, soft, shifting sand between my toes. As the sand got deeper as I walked, it became more difficult to move forward. I was on a road I had never traveled, being in love. I had first fallen in love with Jesus, and now to be in love with my husband and experience a true godly marriage enlightened me and made me radiate as bright as the sun!

As I walked along the beach that beautiful morning, I noticed the birds gathered on the shoreline walking faithfully like they were expecting something great to happen. They seemed to have no worries with their heads held up high in confidence! As if the birds were saying they trusted their creator.

My thoughts focused on these beautiful birds as they confidently walked along the shore. I asked myself, "Are they waiting on God's new day and the beautiful rising of the glowing sun?"

The waves were crashing around me; however, I did not seem to hear them at this moment. Here, on the shore, this day, there is no one to look into my eyes or exclaim what they see in me, like my daughter, now in her twenties, had seen in me when she was much younger. I was here, alone, waiting on the sunrise. An audience of one, and oh, yes, the birds.

It's almost time!! I can see the orange glow peeking out from a distance as if it touches the ocean. The two, the ocean and the rising sun, blend together. I stop walking and watch the glow in the sky, anxious for this beautiful production to start! The waves are crashing around me; however, I do not hear them.

There it is!! The beautiful glow reveals itself! The sun is rising, and the minute the sun arises and lights up the sky, the birds soar!! In my spirit, I say, "The birds are dancing as if to say all glory to You, God, for You, God, are Holy, Holy, Holy, God Almighty!!" Even the birds are dancing at the glory of God and His creation!

I felt I was soaring, dancing along with Jesus hand in hand. When I saw the birds all take flight as the sun rose, it made me think, in spite of all the circumstances that are going on in our lives, God is constant. We get to trust God all along the way during the soars and the waiting, during the flights and the landings, and during the mountaintops and the valleys. God is with us always!

I walk a little farther, focusing and looking up at the sun, and I wipe the tears from my eyes as I wipe the sand off my feet. My feet feel as if they have been lifted, if only for a moment. I climb the steps to our oceanfront room, open the door, and hug my amazing husband, Moe. I lean to give him a sweet kiss and I whisper, "I love you, Honey." He gently takes a hold of my hand that fits perfectly inside his and he looks into my eyes and says, "I love you too, Honey." I feel his heartbeat beating in my hand as our hands are clenched in perfect fit.

He asks me, looking deeply into my eyes, as if he already knows, "How was your walk on the beach, Honey?" I look deeply into his eyes, as if my spirit is telling me to memorize his voice and remember his eyes. I respond, "It was beautiful, Honey. It was beautiful." Even though his body is tired, he says, "It looks like a perfect day for fishing, let's go!" Hand in hand we walk, fishing rods and tackle in one hand, hands clenched. We walk forward, ready to face each step whether soft as sand or hard as pavement. We walk hand in hand.

Surely, God would not allow my life to be shattered again when finally, the pieces seemed to be back together.

We, being newlyweds and so in love, are faced with a new journey that is flaming around our hearts. This new journey demands much attention and is fierce with darts of fire. However, we are holding on to our life and our dreams with every ounce of our beating hearts!

The following pages ebb and flow much like the waves in the ocean. Along my life, there are crossroads of hope and hopelessness, times of belief and disbelief, times of plenty and lacking, times of fear and doubt and courage and faith, and times of shifting sand and steady ground.

God led me to write many journal entries, especially during this time. I simply held the pen and God filled the pages. I didn't know God was writing a book, but God did. It is as if God poured paint onto a blank canvas and God painted the portrait. Me, the penholder, by myself, would not do much with the pen or the paint; however, God makes beauty from ashes. It is amazing to look back at the writings and see God's hand in healing my heart.

God made our hearts and He will heal our hearts in times of heart damage, if we ask! Jesus is here for us, His hands are outstretched toward us, and He is in the healing/transforming business!

When our bodies need physical healing, we often choose a specialist. For healing our hurting hearts, who better than God, who made our heart, to heal our heart? He is certainly a specialist at knowing how He designed our heart and what is needed for our healing from past hurts.

At times of my life, I listened to the best paths for dealing with my past hurts, and at times, I did not turn an ear. I have learned many lessons and have many to learn ahead of me. I started with praying for God to open my heart.

The journey ahead of lies, loss, and finally love meets the journey of restoration, redemption, and refinement through the guidance and love of my Savior, Jesus Christ.

I honestly thought the chains of hurts, lies, and loss from my past that wrapped around me would never break! But God is about shaking and breaking those chains through transformation!

We are all on a journey. I believe we are on a journey here on earth to heaven. We can experience God moments along the way! I pray as you read *And The Birds Danced*, you will see and know the hope found in Jesus.

Does it take a vision from God to start developing your relationship with Jesus? It can, but no, it does not take a vision to begin or deepen your relationship with God. When I was hurting the most, I was still looking for God, even though I was not aware I was looking.

The following chapters share my journal entries and practical ideas to "take the next step" to give you ideas to grow further in your relationship with God. God gives us all HOPE, hope that helps us hold onto the promise of eternity, even among shattered hearts. I pray you enjoy *And The Birds Danced*.

Love, Debra

Chapter 1

In My Own Little World

My teacher described me as "living in my own little world" to my mom at the teacher/parent conference in the small classroom that smelled of chalkboards and erasers. I would say this kindergarten teacher was a wise woman. Looking concerned, she told my mom that I seemed to be "dreaming" during class. I imagine I was coloring outside the lines for sure! Thankfully, broken crayons still color.

I remember Mrs. Buttner, my kindergarten teacher, had a smile that would light up the room. She spoke softly to me and was so sweet. I watched her write on the chalkboard with such ease, holding the starch white chalk firmly. When she made a rare mistake on the chalkboard, she would so elegantly erase the mistake, as if to say, "Look how easily mistakes can be erased." Looking back now, I wish some areas of my life had been erased. I imagine we all would like to elegantly erase some areas of our lives. I wonder if we did grab the eraser, who would we be?

I am blessed with a great family; a mom, dad, and brothers who love and support me. I had love and support from my grandparents, aunts, uncles, and cousins. I loved spending time with my grandparents, each with the strength of a firmly planted oak tree. I have such fond precious memories of my time with my grandparents. Love was all around me; so why was I so sad with such dislike for myself?

I had no idea of the journey my life would take. A life full of believing lies in my mind of my unworthiness. I suppose the imaginary world of dreaming, like Mrs. Buttner had described, seemed easier to me.

When I was small, my older brothers made fun of me, as siblings will do. They even made fun of my kindergarten teacher's name every time I would excitedly share what I had colored in class that day. I am sure being picked on by your siblings is very normal; however, I seemed to overreact to being "picked on." I just wanted to be left alone most of the time. I became very shy as the days grew from one into another. I did not understand why I wanted to be left alone so much.

When I was young, I had a babysitter named Kellan (not his real name for confidentiality). I thought Kellan, being a teenager, was a cool guy until one evening Kellan told me to do something I thought sounded strange.

One day when Kellan was babysitting me, he asked me to undress and run in front of our large front bay window of our house. I looked at Kellan, frightened. Kellan, while laughing loudly, told me, "It would be funny." I had a sick feeling in the pit of my stomach. Kellan raised his voice and said, "If you don't do as I say, I will tell your parents you misbehaved while they were gone." Being four years of age and wanting to listen to and please Kellan, I undressed quickly and ran as fast as I could in front of the front bay window, praying no one saw me. Kellan, laughing, told me to run again! I grabbed my clothes and ran upstairs to get dressed, carrying the heavy sick feeling in my stomach. Kellan laughed hysterically at me.

After I dressed and came slowly down the stairs of our split- level home, Kellan, laughing still, reminded me again I was not to tell my parents about this "run and dodge game" that sickened me.

Often, when Kellan would babysit, he would want to play a "wrestling game." Kellan would hold me down and demand I wrestle him. I didn't even know what wrestling was, and I despised this! He would then spray me with a water bottle until I was drenched in water. He thought that was so funny. I felt more and more worthless and sad.

I would beg my parents to not leave the house the occasional times they would need to hire a babysitter. Once, when my parents were going to their square dancing class, I cried as they left the house. I then literally ran out of the house as they were backing out of the driveway and I ran after their car! I remember running behind their car as fast as I could, chasing them up the road, begging them not to leave. They stopped the car and put me inside of it. Knowing how much I loved going with them to their square dancing classes, they drove me back to the house, assuring me I could go to the next square dance class with them.

I did enjoy going with them to their square dancing classes, especially listening to Mr. Cleller, the square dance caller. He sounded like a singer as he called the square dancing moves with such precision. At the end of class, he would sometimes let me square dance with my parents after sitting on the bleachers, where I had been tapping my toes to the beat of the music and watching every move! I had learned the "dosey doe" call and many other calls, so I was ready to square dance! It was so much fun, and I felt so welcomed and had a sense of belonging! Maybe this led to my love of clogging, which I started also when I was younger.

I loved going to Shoney's Restaurant after each square dance class with my parents and their dancing friends. They always included me and were so kind. So, yes, I loved going places with my parents; however, the fear of my parents leaving was intense inside of me at times.

The night I chased them, pleading with them to take me with them, I had intense fear inside me. I could feel my heart beating out of my chest, even before running as fast as my feet would take me chasing their car! As my parents reached the destination of our house after driving me around the block, I held my head down and slowly walked back into the house. I kept quiet and put my mask of compliance on.

Pleading with my parents to take me with them each time they would leave continued; however, I had stopped chasing their car each time, which must have given them a sense of relief! I remained quiet about Kellan to everyone. I was thankful when Kellan moved away and I did not need a babysitter anymore.

I felt a sense of belonging mostly when I was alone in my own little world. I wanted to be alone, yet at the same time, I wanted to always be in the presence and protection of my parents. My parents were my safety net.

As I went through my teenage years, I found comfort in food and I struggled with the fear of being overweight. My mom told me she was determined I would not have a weight problem and she would keep an eye on my eating. So, the scale became an idol to me. Even when I was at a healthy weight, I saw myself as being very overweight. I felt comforted when I ate and liked eating alone. During my teenage years, I did not have a problem with gaining weight, although in my mind, I was overweight. The true weight gain would come during my first marriage, which I will discuss in the following chapters. Turning to food caught up with me years later. The obsession with the scale caused yet another cycle of lies in my mind and yes, more shattered dreams of being "perfect" like the other girls my age. This created a cruel circle of lies and what seemed like an endless cycle of brokenness.

Growing up, I compared myself to every girl I met and wished I could be like them. To me, each girl I met seemed to be perfect and had their life together. They seemed outgoing, pretty, and confident to me.

I wished I was someone else. I would think to myself, "I wish I was outgoing, pretty, and confident." It didn't matter who I was; I just wanted to be different. I wanted to be someone I could understand. I can look back now and see how I was questioning how God made me, as if He made a mistake knitting me together. It is such a blessing now to know, without a doubt, God makes no mistakes how he wonderfully designs us. We are all beautifully and wonderfully made! We are God's delight!

When I was a teenager, I noticed others talking about dating. I was so intimidated by guys; besides, I did not think I was pretty enough for anyone to date me. I wanted to be to myself in my own little world that was safe. I did not understand why I wanted to be to myself so much. I did not understand me. If a guy would show me attention, I would shy away.

While I was growing up, I was drawn to people who were hurting or people who felt unnoticed. Maybe I was drawn to them because they reminded me of myself, or maybe they were in their own little world also. Maybe, they were introverted like me.

Maybe, I felt different because I was the baby of the family. I didn't know why I wanted to be alone. I could not figure myself out. I had a desire to be "normal" like others.

Because of this desire to be different than I was, I had an imaginary friend named Cindi. I often spoke to Cindi, and it was during this time that I began to be teased even more. I thought I would fit in better in the world of imagination. Perhaps, this drove my mind into overdrive. I have always been one to overthink, especially when I went through the saddest seasons of my life.

I have often felt broken and drawn to brokenness. I was that girl who picked up the broken shells, wondering why so many people treasure the beautiful perfect shells along the shore, when I find beauty in the broken.

I believed I did not measure up to the standards others placed on me. I was taking up space in my mind allowing these beliefs to take up residence, allowing one by one, more rooms in my mind to be added, until the lies in my mind could have appeared on the largest real estate property list!

Besides my own mind, I was allowing circumstances that happened in my life to seemingly take away hope and replace it with, "Oh well, that just happened, reactive living" so to speak. Thankfully, even through my stubbornness , God did not give up on me and allow me to stay at this place and own a country named "The Country of Mind Lies" with a sign boldly exclaiming, "No vacancy, all the property in this country is taken." What an exhausting country that would be!

Jesus began opening my eyes when I turned to him in prayer at the young age of twelve when my grandpa died. I prayed to God, and then I put God back in His box until I would need him again.

When I think of how unworthy I felt through my younger years, I am reminded of the story in the Bible of the Samaritan woman at the well from John 4:4-30[3], one of my favorites. I am reminded of how unworthy the woman at the well must have felt.

I envision the woman at the well. I imagine it was a day like any other day. She walked to a familiar place she had gone so many times with her heart shattered in pieces, feeling so unworthy. She went to the well hoping no one would be there. She hoped to not see anyone. She felt she didn't fit in or measure up to what others thought she should be. She thought it was just another day for her to be laughed at and ridiculed by "the perfect ones" who often were there. She didn't need anyone to make her feel smaller than she felt herself.

Was she seeking more for herself as she walked to the well this day? She didn't even think there should be more for her. As you see, she felt so unworthy.

So, she traveled to the well during a time of the day that no one would be there, putting one foot in front of the other like any other ordinary day.

Little did she know that today would be different! She was about to be made new and to be changed! Does this make the

---

3 NIV, See footnotes.

"used to be" her of no value? I think not. I believe the person she used to be had a desire to become something new that would be valued even more.

For you see, this day, she met a man at the well who saw her, and he cared about her. He saw more in her, more than she knew existed.

This man who saw more of her asked her for a drink from the well. She reminded him he should not speak to her, since she was a Samaritan woman. She was focusing on the law of Jews not speaking to Samaritans, but he was focused on love and grace. This man fired embers of HOPE inside her.

He introduced her to real love, real living water. She found out this man is the Messiah! He showed her she was valued and He showed her grace. Once she recognized the greatness of this gift, she felt she had to share it! She, once embarrassed and hidden, ran to share this great news with others!

I can relate to the woman at the well feeling unworthy. It gives me hope to see her meeting Jesus in her brokenness. I remind myself Jesus is there waiting for me as well, loving me just as I am.

Would I ever open up and come out of my broken shell? Would I ever soar like a bird, even though my wing has been bruised? Would I one day share that Jesus knows me and loves me just as I am?

Growing up, I learned some unhealthy coping mechanisms, especially when new challenges occurred. I also wanted to hide like the woman at the well.

I would find myself turning to food or focusing on how I didn't fit in with my cousins or my friends. It was as if I was saying, "Do not speak to me, I am not worthy." I was wondering what I needed to do to fit in or how I was supposed to look, or who would laugh at me today?

I imagine others probably go through this "trying to figure yourself out stage." For me, I found staying in my "own little world" made me feel safe. Maybe, that was just easier for me and the easy way out of the difficult work of uncovering deep secrets and hurts. I am thankful for God's never-ending grace and God didn't give up on me! Even amid our broken shattered pieces, God sees us, loves us, and knows us!

God showed me even though my dream when I was younger of being like the others who seemed "normal" (although not sure what normal is) was shattered, there was still beauty in the ashes of my untrue thoughts of myself. God showed me this by revealing I could start talking to Him right where I was, who I was, without judgment. God wants us to communicate with Him and be real. God knows us and wants to hear the details of our desires and thoughts. Even when we don't know what to say, just say to God, "God, let others see You in me today," even among our own possible feelings of unworthiness.

Starting our prayers with thankfulness is a great start also. "Thank you, God, for the breath you breathe into us."

I was glad my parents had taken me to Sunday School and church at a young age. I saw how active my parents were in church, and they radiated love for each other and love for others. My parents showed me unconditional love, accepting me right where I was. I, however, had kept secrets from them because I felt it was best to not talk about "problems." So, I did not share about my insecurities or about how I was treated by Kellan, the babysitter.

The following are writings about my feelings of unworthiness, my mindset of believing lies, and some of the scriptures and inspirations that encouraged me as I began becoming aware of the layers that were awaiting to be peeled away and discovered within myself. I often wondered if people did not have pain, would they experience healing or know what comfort truly is?

It took a journey through childhood into adulthood for me to believe a life of unconditional love without judgment was even available for me! Jesus was there to take hold of the eraser (when I allowed him to) and erase the pathway in my mind of lies about myself that I was less than a broken penny crushed into the pavement.

The more I prayed and reached out to Jesus, the more I started getting closer to a new pathway to truth, hope, and unconditional love. I was worthy of a new slate wiped clean and a new beginning. Would I stay on this path even among more broken dreams?

You will find at the end of each chapter of *And The Birds Danced* my personal journal writings. They reveal times I called out to God in complete rawness and in pain. Like David, the shepherd boy who became king in the Bible, I also cried out in lament to God, as well as times I thanked God for His faithfulness. In my journal writings, like the ebb and flow of the ocean waves, there are writings about thankfulness, faithfulness, hope, despair, desire, pain, belief, disbelief, discovery, and awareness.

In our lives, we may feel we are standing on a steady unmovable rock at times full of certainty and confidence or, we may feel we are sinking deeply into shifting sand. We may be at a crossroads, not knowing which way to turn, or which way the road will turn as we stand, waiting and wondering about our future.

We may feel we are in a huge wave as big as a tsunami about to crash and take us under! Often, however, it is inside the storms of our lives we begin discovery! The calm seasons of our lives may provide time to build our foundation of faith, and the storms allow time for true discovery as we become aware of how we need our Savior, Jesus.

We may feel we are the broken seashell or the beautiful shell without a flaw, like God sees beauty in us. We may feel we are inside a huge wave of a storm that is engulfing us. If so, ask God to show you how you are protected by His love. "Help us, Lord!" we cry.

God surrounds us even as we are engulfed in the wave. We may see the wave as frightening. We may strive to look to the shore that represents the destination of peace we are striving for. In striving ahead, know that God never wastes a hurt, and we will not stay in this wave forever. Envision where your peace comes from, and tomorrow, repeat envisioning where your peace comes from.

Just a reminder, whichever season you may be in, be kind to yourself. Just take the next right step, holding on to God, and try to see the protection of the shore in spite of the wave. The journey is not a huge leap. It is one small step at a time, or one wave at a time.

Think about the last time you were at the beach. When I was growing up, we spent some time vacationing at the beach. I would love to stand close to the shore and jump as high as my young feet would jump over each wave that came unto the shore. My dad saw how much I loved jumping the waves, and he would pick me up, hold me close, and walk out farther into the ocean to "catch" the bigger waves as they came in from the ocean. We walked closer to meet the bigger waves, and as long as I was in the arms of my dad, I felt safe and found delight in the huge waves! I felt I could face them as long as I was in the arms of my dad, my father who I trusted! After a while, I was happy to go back to my small waves by the shore by myself and jump over them.

I think about my life now during times of facing the huge waves of the unknowns, including the ones that might knock me down. Much like when my dad scooped me up, held me close, and walked with me out to meet the big waves in the ocean when I was small, God, our Father, scoops us up and walks with us to meet the big waves. God sometimes allows us to stay for a while along the shore, jumping the small waves by ourselves. Whether along the shore or walking out to meet the big waves, God, our Father, is walking alongside us!

Aren't you glad you do not have to jump all the waves in the vast ocean at one time? God knows to bring just one wave at a time. When you see waves, some waves are bigger than others, but they were all designed for that moment. Treasure each moment. Even the painful moments have purpose. Even if one knocks you down, you raise up and are better prepared for the next wave, knowing where your help comes from. Our help comes from our beloved Savior!

At times, when I sensed hurt coming into my life, or fear of hurt, I ran and hid, which could be referred to as "flight." When I ran and hid and buried my feelings in the sand, my mind sometimes went into retreat. It seemed odd that I was drawn to people who felt they were unnoticed; however, I didn't mind avoiding my own unnoticed feelings. In this retreat of hiding, I envisioned a cleft that felt safe. I could almost envision a huge cleft that had "Debra's Cleft Just for Her" engraved in stone. I felt if I was in my safe cleft alone, no one could hurt me there. I didn't see that running to a safe zone was truly hurting me more. I was digging my hurts or fears of being hurt deeper and deeper into the sand.

I enjoy learning new things, especially about animals. My fun, whimsical friend Bea loves birds. She also loves to read. Her face lights up when she shares with me a "fun fact." She is one of those friends who makes you feel better about everything after talking with her.

Bea recently told me a fun fact about white pelicans. She learned that white pelicans enjoy dining alone on the fish they catch. When they drain their pouches after catching fish, other sea birds sometimes try to steal their food from the pelican's mouth. Can you imagine catching a fish, only to have it snatched away when you were just trying to seek nourishment?

Do you at times identify with the pelican? Do you sometimes feel you are on your journey of life and at times, the world just takes and takes from you, leaving you desiring to be left alone?

The Lord pursues us, yes, even when we desire to be left alone.

Truth is, as we journey along the way, God is there, was there, and will be there.

Along my journey, am I the person I would like to be? Not even. However, I am not the person I was. I am growing in my relationship with Jesus, trusting him along the way to help me turn from a mindset of victimization to a mindset of acceptance in being victorious in Jesus!

Like the white pelican, I am seeking nourishment. At times, I feel like being alone and retreating to a cleft of safety. I am thankful God pursues me.

With the love of my Father, God, His son, Jesus, and the guidance of the Holy Spirit, all three in one, I too can run to tell of the transformation from a little girl who stayed in her own little world to proclaiming she is a member of the royal court as being a daughter of the King! She can announce to the world about the love of Jesus, the one she met one day who knew her and loved her as she was and as she is.

We are all children of God, loved and known members of His royal court! His love is a gift for all who accept and open His gift of hope and eternal life living with Jesus in heaven when we are called to our forever home.

Journal Entries, Scriptures, and Inspirations

Broken, Blessed, Beaten, Beauty. Can these all be possible during one season of our lives?

"Father God, help me to stop comparing. Help me to learn from the bloom of a flower that does not compare itself to other flowers. A flower blooms. Help me, God, to bloom where you want me; as you want me."

Psalm 59:16 (NIV) "But I will sing of your strength, in the morning I will sing of your love, for you are my fortress, my refuge in times of trouble."[4]

"She's the Girl"

She's the girl by the ocean in her jeans. She's the girl at the summer baseball game covered by her coat.

She's the girl staring at her photograph, feeling ashamed.

She's the girl who can envision others talking of how she let herself go.

She's the girl who never measures up in her mind.

---

4 NIV, See footnotes

She's the girl who, as a child, was given a promise to never weigh more than she should.

She's the girl who was told by others that she was getting fat.

She's the girl who hid from the others, ashamed.

She's the girl who allowed herself to look at the number on the scale as she weighed herself to determine how she felt for the day.

She's the girl who stayed home and missed her prom.

She's the girl who covered her heart.

Still, She's the Girl

And she asks, "God, how did you make my heart?" And she listens.

She's the girl who God knit together;
> Who God loves;
> Who God treasures;
> Who God defines as His, as she is.
> God covers her in His love and mercy;
> God covers her in His kindness and His grace;
> God covers her in His abundance and His truth;
> God covers her in His promises and His heart.

> She is the girl, a new creation!
> God's girl, fully known and loved!
> She is sealed as God's girl!

Psalm 139 (The Message) [5]

"God, investigate my life; get all the facts firsthand.
I'm an open book to you; even from a distance, you know
what I'm thinking.
You know when I leave and when I get back; I'm never out of
your sight.
You know everything I'm going to say before I start the first
sentence.
I look behind me and you're there, then up ahead and you're
there, too;
your reassuring presence, coming and going.
This is too much, too wonderful—
I can't take it all in!

Is there any place I can go to avoid your Spirit,
to be out of your sight?
If I climb to the sky, you're there!
If I go underground, you're there!
If I flew on morning's wings
 to the far western horizon,
You'd find me in a minute—
 you're already there waiting!

Then I said to myself, "Oh, he even sees me in the dark!"
At night I'm immersed in the light!
It's a fact; darkness isn't dark to you;
night and day, darkness and light, they're all the same to you.

---

5 The Message Bible, See footnotes.

Oh yes, you shaped me first inside, then out;
you formed me in my mother's womb.
I thank you, High God—you're breathtaking!
Body and soul, I am marvelously made
I worship in adoration—what a creation!
You know me inside and out,
you know every bone in my body;
You know exactly how I was made, bit by bit,
how I was sculpted from nothing into something.
Like an open book, you watched me grow from conception to birth;
all the stages of my life were spread out before you,
The days of my life all prepared;
before I'd even lived one day.

Your thoughts—how rare, how beautiful!
God, I'll never comprehend them!
I couldn't even begin to count them—
any more than I could count the sand of the sea.
Oh, let me rise in the morning and live always with you!
And please, God, do away with wickedness for good!
And, you murderers—out of here!—
all the men and women who belittle you, God,
infatuated with cheap god-imitations.

See how I hate those who hate you, God,
see how I loathe all this godless arrogance.
I hate it with pure, unadulterated hatred.
Your enemies are my enemies!

Investigate my life, O God;

find out everything about me.
Cross-examine and test me;
get a clear picture of what I'm about.
See for yourself whether I've done anything wrong—
then guide me on the road to eternal life."

Heal Me, God from the Inside Out

I love you more than all the grains of sand in the world and way way more is what I tell my children. Guess what? God tells us the same! We are the proud picture He shows because we belong. We belong to God. God created you and He loves you! He knows the number of hairs on your head! He knows you and yet, he still loves you. Ask God, "God, how did you make my heart?"; then, be still and listen. You will be amazed!!

Psalm 94:18 (NIV) When I said, "My foot is slipping," your unfailing love, Lord, supported me.[6]

Psalm 94:19 (NIV) "When anxiety was great within me, your consolation brought me joy, Lord."[7]

Colossians 1:17 (NIV) "He is before all things, and in Him all things hold together."[8]

---

6 NIV, See footnotes.
7 NIV, See footnotes.
8 NIV, See footnotes.

"The Backpack of Stones"

On my back, you see, I carry a book bag.
Along life's way, I can choose what I carry.
I begin with love, thankfulness, gratitude, and kindness
Of these, I feel so much comfort.

As I travel my path set before me, I encounter a few new paths;
these seem unfamiliar.
Some of these paths I chose, some others entice.
My backpack has room left; I pick up and add: distraction,
blinders, weight added I feel;
Hurt, not to be left out, jumps in. The weight on my back! Oh,
how heavy! Carrying all this hurts!

As I travel now with more weight and burdens to bear
There is a new distraction that weighs heavy as a boulder.
Did I ignore the dreams I thought were set out for me?
What happened to the comfort and peace? "Where is peace?",
I cry!

As I travel, there is one who has been by my side and remained
steadfast, although at times, my own path I sought.
His eyes quietly tear up and tears roll down upon His face
As you see, I chose to see the rocks and gravels along the path
instead of His hand to take a hold.
"Lie down that book bag of heavy boulders, my child" He lovingly says.

I have carried it all for you
As I traveled the path to Calvary, my love for you always.
My hands I gave for nails reach out to guide your way.

For as we travel our path of life; hand in hand, along the way, come what may,
Jesus and me, our heartbeats in hand will stand for eternity!

I have always enjoyed Janet Eggleston's poem, "It's In the Valleys I Grow," especially these verses:

"Sometimes life seems hard to bear,
Full of sorrow, trouble and woe,
It's then I have to remember
That it's in the valley I grow.

If I always stayed on the mountain top,
And never experienced pain,
I would never appreciate God's love
And would be living in vain."[9]

Prayer: *Father God, thank you for your love; a love so deep and wide, it's hard for us to imagine. Help us to shake off anything that trips or hinders us from knowing the love given by you, our Rock and Redeemer. Clear our minds and place us on pathways that lead to you, and remind us you travel alongside us. We are not alone! Let our path be cleared of any stones, boulders, or temptations that could cause our steps to venture away from your path, Lord. Help us to be your hands, feet, heart, and*

9 See Footnotes.

mind. We love you and we thank you. Our hope is found in you, Lord. In your precious Son's name, Jesus, we pray. Amen.

"Waiting is our destiny, as creatures who cannot by themselves bring about what they hope for; we wait in the darkness for a flame we cannot light. We wait in fear for a happy ending that we cannot write. We wait for a 'not yet' that feels like a 'not ever'"
—LEWIS SMEDES [10]

Often, when I call out to God, it brings comfort, peace, and hope. I find it amazing to look back at journal entries and see how God answers prayers.

Hope[11] is defined as a noun as, "A desire accompanied by expectation of or belief in fulfillment." As a verb, hope is explained as, "To cherish a desire with anticipation; wanting something to happen or be true."

When we ask God for a desire of our heart, God may answer with not now, maybe later, wait, or yes. Often, just talking with God gives me a feeling of not being alone.

I wonder, at times, if my journal entries I wrote were drawing me from lies in my mind to a secure place of hope and love found in Jesus Christ. I thought I was pouring out to God my desires, and actually, all along, God was revealing to me who I truly am.

---

10 See footnotes.
11 See footnotes.

Healthy relationships involve communicating with each other. I believe talking to God makes us active participants in our faith. Often, I find a quiet place to help deter any distractions. I remind myself to remember to listen also for the guidance of the Holy Spirit. Envision your conversation with God!

Notes/How This Applies:

At the end of each chapter, feel free to include any notes you would like to make or illustrations if you enjoy drawing. Just be you.:-)

Take the Next Step Idea: Envision an eagle soaring! Research flights and landings of eagles. Where is a new area you would like to soar? Ask God to show you His path for you. Ask God to provide opportunities in His will to travel together on this new flight.

When I think of eagles' flights, I imagine God's strength to renew people and give them strength to soar. God is able to take the weariest to new heights unimaginable!

It is amazing to look back at prayers and see God's wonderment.

Take The Next Step Idea: Start a prayer journal by journaling prayer requests and /or praises. If you enjoy drawing, consider drawing your prayers and/or praises. Consider including a date when you make your prayer journal entry or drawing.

And/or consider starting a prayer closet. Write prayers or praises on sticky notes. Place your prayer request or praise that is written on your sticky note and place it on your wall in your prayer closet. As God answers your prayers, you can move the sticky note to another area. Remember, even if you leave your sticky note in its original position, God is working.

Sometimes, when I think my life is over, I learn it might just be an entry to a new beginning with God. Embrace and envision trusting God deeper, right where you are.

Pain, hurt, and disappointment can place your feet on the bridge to trusting God deeper. Take the next step as you move closer to Jesus! He is holding the bridge up firmly and walking alongside you! We get to trust God!

Chapter 2

Looking For The Shore Beyond The Waves

In my life, I have wasted a lot of time waiting for the good seasons of my life to end. During that mindset, the pathway of low self-worth grew.

The ebb and flow of my struggles with anxiety, low self-esteem, comparison, depression, and believing lies in my mind felt like riding in a boat. I would cut loose from holding on to the side of the boat during calm water and grip the side of the boat during the rough waters. These struggles ride the waves, at times, like tsunamis and, at times, lie unnoticed as they come to shore quietly. It is often during the calm waters of my life when I build my faith, and during the rough waters, I begin to discover my faith.

Sometimes, even during the calm seasons, little triggers would raise as if raising up from a deep sand dune that had been lying along the shore! If someone would say a word that would trigger a hurt, up from the sand dune a feeling would scream inside me from a deep dark place!

Hidden in sand dunes, I sometimes find driftwood that has been washed up from the ocean. At times, the driftwood I find is sturdy, and other times, I pick it up and it falls apart. Sometimes, we are fragile like driftwood and one disappointment or feeling of judgment from another person or circumstance that causes hurt can make us feel we are falling apart as well.

I remind myself to remain faithful. Even during the seasons of huge waves of struggles that can sometimes cause me to drift away from God, I strive to see the shore and know God will bring me back into His loving arms, often purified and refined, prepared to anchor into His foundation of unending love.

When my low esteem is the lowest in my life, I struggle with the "overs" and "unders." The "overs" include overthinking, overanalyzing, overspending, overreacting, and overeating. The "unders" in my life are when I am at my lowest, believing I would never matter or measure up. The "unders" could be described as me feeling less than a chipped-off penny crushed into the pavement.

This going from "unders" to "overs" caused a cycle of depression to the point I did not want to leave my home at times. I am thankful these times of "unders" and "overs" do not define me. Often, when my feelings of "unders" were heightened, I would visit the "overs" and overeat, overspend, and overthink to an unhealthy level. Then, the "unders" would appear again. Well, you see the cycle and pattern.

I have become keenly aware that, "I struggle, and I need my Savior each and every day."

We all struggle with something, and as I have said in the past, "If you say you do not struggle with anything, well then, welcome to the struggle of denial." No, the denial I am referring to is not a body of water in Egypt. How wonderful to not be defined by our struggles! How wonderful it is to be defined as being children of God!

Each day, every minute, we have the opportunity to accept a personal relationship with God. God desires a relationship with us. Through this relationship of opening up to God, I met the new me by discovering a growing awareness of the broken me. The broken me began to meet the whole me. The chains of the secret lies that I once believed began to shake!

The secret lies that I was defined by a number on a scale, unloved and worthless, were suffocating the person God made me to be.

It seemed that even when I would turn to God in prayer, I just visited with God until I felt better and more hopeful; then, I would place God back in his box I kept him in.

Have you ever had a wound that was beginning to scab over and heal? I have. I would feel the wound improving and the scab protecting me and then, at times, I would rip the scab off to start the healing process again.

Why do I sometimes do the things I know I should not do? Why do I sometimes not let healing have the time it deserves? Why do I not do the things I know I should do? Even Paul, who was transformed from Saul, asked this question of why he did the things he knew he should not do. Paul says, in

Romans 7:15, "I do not understand what I do. For what I want to do, I do not do, but what I hate, I do."[12]

When I look at some of the struggles and shattered dreams in the Bible, why do I think I should be struggle free? I often turn to the book of Psalms and look at the life of David, who is considered a man after God's own heart. Why was David considered to have this kind of heart? Some of the characteristics I believe that made David's heart a heart that sought God were his desire to follow God's will, his absolute faith in God, his love for God, and his thankfulness and true repentance after he sinned.

I imagine approaching a bridge to a pathway to peace. Approaching with an awareness of a heart for God is a great way to step on that bridge to transformation.

Loving God, praying for His will, strengthening our faith daily, being thankful, and repenting daily of our sins helps us to look forward and strive onward, throwing aside anything that tries to hold us back.

I will share some of my struggles, shattered dreams, and discoveries along my journey that tried and still try to hinder my growth as I try to strive onward to having a heart for God. Looking back, I can see how these struggles opened my eyes to growing my faith and giving hope a voice.

I remember looking at the picture on the wall of the house I grew up in. In the picture, I was no more than the age of two. My blue eyes and blonde hair shined, exhibiting beams of happiness radiating through the glass on the frame! In the picture, my smile, as bright and big as the sunshine, drew me in!

---

12 NIV, See footnotes.

I found myself standing in the hallway of the house I grew up in, in my forties at the time, not knowing this little girl in the picture frame upon the wall of my parents' home, although this little girl was me. I thought, "Oh, how I wish that radiance would shine from within me now and that I would have that same spirit!" I began to cry in the hallway of my homeplace of many years ago. Thankfully, no one was around to see my crying. It was only me and my "used to be" there.

How did I lose that joy that shined from that smile when I was a toddler? I started to feel robbed of dreams and joy. I felt I messed up and didn't measure up. There, standing in the hallway, the bright-eyed younger me seemed to speak to the older me saying, "You had dreams!", "You had a chance!", "Where did you go wrong?" I felt I had made choices that eliminated any dreams of a future. Wow! That was surely giving a lot of power to choices and circumstances! My mind was in overdrive again, believing untruths like I had done before. Here we go, circling around this mountain again!

At my church, I would hear people talk about grace and mercy and I wondered what grace and mercy meant. I was living grace and did not know it. My journey along the way taught me grace. My journey now is still teaching me grace. I know grace now by experiencing grace. It is difficult to show grace to others if you do not show grace to yourself.

Grace[13] is defined as "love and mercy given to us by God because God desires us to have it, not because of anything we have done to earn it." Grace is also defined as "courteous

---

13 See footnotes.

goodwill." "It is not asked for, nor deserved, but is freely given," the definition goes on to say.

Mercy[14] is defined as "the compassion and kindness shown to someone whom it is in one's own power to punish or harm." "It is the act meant to relieve someone of their suffering," the definition goes on to say.

I heard the story of a boy who desired a bike and he, out of desperation for his desire, did something he shouldn't have done. The young boy stole a bicycle from a neighborhood teenager. The teenager caught the boy stealing his bike. The boy, with tears in his eyes, told the teenager, he "didn't mean to do any harm." The teenager chose not to report the theft; instead, he pardoned the boy and let the matter go. Then, the teenager went into his room where he had been keeping money he was saving. He took the money and went to his local department store and bought a new bike. He then presented the brand-new bike to the young boy. This story is a great example of mercy and grace.

Being the youngest child of my family and the only girl made me feel special when I was two years of age as I was in the picture I saw on the wall. It seemed as if I had a highly specialized rank without the effort of being special because I was the baby of the family and the only girl.

My grandparents showed me much love, and they were amazing role models. My grandma (my dad's mom) had a sweet, loving, humble, and Christlike manner of unconditional love, and I treasured spending time with my grandparents.

---

14 See footnotes.

I remember my grandpa's beautiful prayers, and we loved to clog and mountain dance together.

My grandpa (my mom's dad), a retired train engineer, called me his little nurse since I was age twelve. As his health was failing, I loved taking care of my grandpa. Once, during one of his hospitalizations, I grabbed a wheelchair and took Grandpa for a ride down to the gardens outside. He smiled with such happiness. I felt I mattered, and I was valued for something I did on my own. He, along with my grandma, would take me fishing, and I loved spending time on the lake!

When I was young, as discussed earlier, I knew of God from going to church and seeing the love of Christ my parents showed in life.

I thought you prayed when you needed God, so I kept God in a box for times I needed Him. I seemed to go through life without much effort, and I lived life with a reactive, passive method. I learned to keep to myself and keep feelings hidden within me.

My family moved from the town of Rawlings near my birthplace of Cumberland, Maryland, to Lexington, North Carolina, when I was seven years of age because of my dad's job.

I became employed at the age of fifteen working retail. I saved money for my first car! I became focused on working as many hours as I could. I signed up to work, missing many school extracurricular events, and even chose to miss both of my proms. I honestly thought no guy would take me to a dance anyway.

I stopped attending church all together during my teenage years because I didn't feel I fit in with the other youth at my church.

My mom encouraged me to join an organization called The International Order of the Rainbow for Girls, as she was a Rainbow Girl when she was younger. Rainbow Girls is a Masonic youth service organization which teaches leadership, service, and charity to fellow citizens and communities. In this organization, I held "offices" as I traveled through the stations of faith, hope, and charity, worthy associate advisor, and worthy advisor.

Each station in Rainbow Girls involved memory work, which greatly helped me advance out of my shyness in my adolescent years. After moving through the various stations of this organization, I became a worthy advisor. We planned many community events focusing on helping others, and we memorized biblical passages and recited them. I made many great friendships that I still have to this day through this organization. As I continued in this organization, I could feel my confidence start to grow slowly. I held a state office, and an article was in our local newspaper about our state meeting. Upon seeing this, some guys at school would make fun of me, calling me a Rainbow Girl. As I was made fun of, my shyness tried to reappear, demanding attention and telling me to retreat to my old mind of believing untruths about myself. I was glad I was so busy with memory work from Rainbow Girls that I did not have time to think much about these old untruths.

Even though I was a Rainbow Girl, I dreamed of being a princess when I was young. Many young girls dream of that, I imagine. I enjoyed watching romance movies, dreaming of someday my prince showing up. Of course, I liked stories having happy endings! Don't we all like happy endings? My heart grew with a desire for my own love story after each love story I saw!

I was very focused on my weight as a teenager, and once, someone in my family I loved said I was getting fat. I was crushed. I went on a diet, and thought weight was why I was so different and shy. I ate five hundred calories a day and lost weight and felt good about myself when the weight came off. This added to my battle with the scale and my eating misperception.

I graduated from high school and then moved on to nursing school. My parents, being my safety net, now lived several hours away.

My years living away from home had many influential experiences. One, I will never forget.

While I was in nursing school, I was assigned a patient in the hospital who no one wanted as their patient. Our instructor would give us our patient assignments the night before clinicals, and we would go to the hospital unit to research the patient's chart the night before our scheduled clinical day to learn about their medications and their diagnosis.

I walked to the unit with confidence, as I had done many times prior. I found my name on the assignment list and my heart sank!! My eyes saw my assigned patient's diagnosis of AIDS!! At that moment, I didn't even see his name or make note of it. "This patient" was described by others as "giving up." He repeatedly refused to bathe or walk in the hall. Most of the nurses assumed he would not leave his room because of his diagnosis.

When I saw I was assigned this patient, I thought, "Why would my instructor assign me this patient?" Out of all the nursing students, my instructor assigned this patient to me?!

This was in the 1980s, and the fear of being around anyone with AIDS was intense. There was much left to discover about this diagnosis back in those days.

I was so scared of going to clinicals the next day. I researched my patient's chart and his medications, as I knew my nursing instructor would drill me the next morning at our usual preclinical meeting on the nursing floor. But honestly, I was so frightened, my legs were weak walking back to my nursing dorm that was attached to the hospital through a walkway within the hospital.

I reached my dorm room, closed the door, and thought to myself, "Just call in sick and don't go tomorrow!" But, the thought of lying and not showing up to clinicals gave me a sick feeling that was worse than the feeling of my heart sinking earlier.

The last time I talked to God was when I was twelve years old when my grandpa died. It seemed I had two types of praying: passive or reactive. I could be described as a "cause and effect praying person," I imagine. Again, I displayed the mentality of God being in a box on an "as needed basis," similar to a genie in a bottle.

This particular night, when I saw I was assigned this patient I was fearful of caring for, I took God out of that closed box I had kept him in. I prayed for God to give me strength and for me to look through the lens of Jesus when I saw this patient. I told God about my fear. Then, a peace came over me about going to clinicals the next day.

The next morning came. I put my nursing student blue and white uniform on, firmly pinned my dovetail nursing cap on top of my head, and made the long walk to the unit. I met my instructor and other student nurses for the preclinical meeting. My nursing instructor, Ms. Beamstar, asked us questions as if she was a drill sergeant being watched trying for her next rank of promotion!

I answered my instructor's questions, being glad she could not see the anxiety building inside me as I felt beads of sweat forming on my forehead. Her "drills" made me envision me wearing heavy army boots walking through the trenches of deep dark mud, instead of me wearing my good-supported starch white nursing shoes! I honestly felt I was standing on sinking sand; however, I stood confidently as she asked me my goals for my patient that day. I answered her, trying to keep my voice from shaking, and said, "I hope to take care of his ADLs (Activities of Daily Living) and that he will walk with me in the hallway today." My instructor raised her eyebrow and dismissed my answer, and she went on to drilling the next student. My firm, fastened feet held to the blocked tile floor not swaying, as I did not want to show this particular instructor my fears.

After drilling all of us, Ms. Beamstar, holding her steaming hot cup of coffee, gave her young nursing students a firm salute and dismissed us with our caring compassionate hearts onward to care for our patients.

My knees, already weak, made the walk from the nurses' station down the long white hallway to my patient's room, still doubtful of myself. One of the nurses on the floor passed me in the long hallway and sweetly smiled at me and said, "Let me know if you need me today," as if she still remembered being a student nurse herself. I smiled and thanked her.

I slowly opened the big brown heavy door into my patient's dimly lit room. I introduced myself and told him I would be his student nurse. We talked for a while. Well, mostly, I did the talking. I encouraged him to get a bath, and he shook his head, saying "No."

I told him, "Since I am a student nurse, if I tell my nursing instructor you refused your bath today, she will give me a bad grade." She is like that, so I really wish you would get a bath; besides, this soap smells amazing! He and his partner, who was by his bedside, laughed, and he said, "Well OK, I don't want you to get a bad grade."

I got to wash his feet and talk with him. Later in the day, I asked him about taking a walk with me in the hallway. Much to my surprise, he said, "Yes, Debra, thank you. It would be nice to get out of these four walls for a while" We ventured out into the hospital hallway, much like venturing out into the unknowns of this world, us both frightened of what was ahead.

As we walked, my patient took a hold of my hand. I gave his hand a squeeze, as if to say, "I care and I value you, my new friend." We walked several laps around the hospital floor holding hands. As we walked by the nurses' station, you could see the look of surprise from the nurses on the floor that my new friend was out of his room. I know I had a beam of radiance that glowed from my face as we walked by the nurses' station, as if to be announcing, "I am so proud and happy I was chosen to be his student nurse!" My new friend's name was forever ingrained into my heart. I saw his name, I knew his name, and I saw him as a beloved child of God. I no longer saw his diagnosis. I knew him, and we were both blessed beyond borders.

At the end of my shift that day, upon meeting with my instructor at the post clinical meeting, I asked Ms. Beamstar to please assign me the same patient for the entire week! And she did! What a blessed week that was!

This sweet man, still to this day, thirty-six years later, has a place in my heart. He taught me so much. I remember seeing him as a child of God, and this was one of the first times I truly felt compassion for another person who was not in my family. I learned by accepting yourself and showing yourself grace, you gain a perspective to accept others for where they are and who they are through Jesus' vision.

About a year later, I was at a grocery store in Charlotte, North Carolina and my patient's partner was there. He came up to me, called me by name, and gave me the biggest hug. I asked about my patient. He said he had passed away. He said, "Debra, you were so special to him and to me, and he thought so much of you." I told him what a positive impact they both were to me and how I was blessed by meeting both of them! He asked me how nursing school was going and he wished me much happiness. We hugged and he told me God sure had called me to the right profession.

I give all glory to God for the lesson I learned that day. I still remember what an impact this had on my nursing career and on myself as a person. I am so glad God gave me the courage to go to clinicals that day!

Three years from the day I moved into nursing school, I became a registered nurse, which greatly blessed my life! It seemed my patients gave me a purpose for my life. I knew, without a doubt, this was a perfect match for my career, or as I like to say, it was a great heart match. Nursing is so much more than a career, it is my DNA. I love being a nurse! I am still being blessed with heart connections with many new friends I make as a nurse.

As my nursing school graduation was approaching, my oldest brother introduced me to Lyle, a man who was eight years older than myself. Lyle went to church and sent me roses. It was during a time that, in my mind, I was the last single girl left on the face of the earth! So, I said, "Yes" when Lyle asked me out for a date. I also figured others thought it was time I dated. Once again, I was putting more value to others' thoughts than my own.

There were many red flags that became red banners as we dated for several months that I buried in the sand. Thinking this was my only chance of becoming a wife and maybe I would grow to love Lyle, I said, "Yes" when he asked me to marry him. Then, he pulled out a gumball machine ring he thought was funny. Later, a real ring appeared. He said he loved me, and I responded, "You do?" I ignored the many red flags that later became red banners. My friends and other nurses at the hospital I was working at told me I did not seem excited about getting married. One of the nurses wanted to set me up on a date with her son; however, I told her no, I was engaged.

I literally had a sick feeling in my stomach the day before I married Lyle, and the sick feeling remained, even on our trip after the wedding. At the exact time I almost called the wedding to Lyle off, he sent me roses.

The next day, my wedding day, I felt the invisible mask that was on my face as I put on my wedding dress. I walked down the aisle to a lie and began the pretending game. After all, I had learned to keep my struggles to myself. Besides, everyone had this on their plans for the day. I also thought this was probably my only chance to be a wife.

I pretended to be happy and began a life of hiding. I would quickly validate that others had it worse and carry on about my days. My sadness resonated with people who knew me.

I felt I couldn't do anything right as a young bride. During my first marriage to Lyle, my heart tried to fall in love with him, however I could not force love. I became sadder and sadder . Our marriage was less than ideal. Although I cared for Lyle, it was clear the only growth in our marriage was in the number of years only. As our years grew in marriage, I once again retreated to hiding my feelings and keeping my sadness to myself. Lyle and myself grew further apart.

One day, I met Arie. Arie had such a sweet spirit, with such sad eyes that had black and blue bruises around them. She shyly told me with tears streaming down her face that she had been married to Brandt nine years, and sometimes, Brandt would drink too much alcohol and hit her. She made excuses saying, "He just didn't know what he was doing when he overdrank." The sadness in her eyes spoke pain. My heart ached for Arie as I sat with her holding her hand. I asked her what I could do to help. She responded with tears flowing, "Please, just pray he stops drinking."

I had never prayed with someone before out loud; however, I took God out of my box that I kept him in, and I prayed with Arie right then. Her head lifted after we prayed together, and her bruised eyes began to show hope. By sharing, being open, and talking, we became lifelong friends.

People who are being physically abused can sometimes show outward bruises and sometimes, their wounds are hidden deep within them. While I was offering support to Arie just listening to her and showing I cared, I would whisper to myself, "See, at least you are not being physically beaten by Lyle. I would tell myself to just keep trying to do better and maybe someday, you will measure up and be the wife Lyle wanted. I was not being my true self. I would have people come up to me and say, "I just want you to know I see and I am praying for you." I wondered what they saw. Now, I know they saw the sadness streaming through the pretending. They saw the real me deep down inside, pushing and pulling the walls of my true heart to escape.

When we went out in public, Lyle would tell jokes. Oh, he did have a great sense of humor. We had some good times early on in our marriage when we would ride the tractor together, build snowmen, and make the best onion rings every time it snowed. But, I never was in love with Lyle.

As my sadness and darkness became stronger, I became closer to God. I attended many opportunities at church to learn about this God who seemed to respond when I talked with Him.

As I read God's word more, I felt Jesus inviting me to a closer, deeper relationship with Him.

With my past of thinking I didn't measure up, reading God's word began to give me hope I had not felt before. I began to talk to God more through prayer to give me peace and ease my mind from over analyzing my thoughts. I was also tired of pretending to have feelings that were not there for Lyle. I believe God was healing my heart one piece at a time .

Since I was quiet about my life, I had only one person to turn to—the one I kept in my "as needed box." I took God out of His box and I started to pray more again because I knew it had worked while I was in nursing school.

Lyle and I became pregnant and did suffer a miscarriage years after our marriage. I sobbed at the loss of our baby. Lyle was very supportive of me during this time. He told me, "We will have a baby, don't worry." Lyle was right. We gave birth to a healthy baby boy that showed me how deep love is! God went on to bless us with two beautiful daughters.

It was nice to see this side of Lyle. Lyle and I were blessed with three amazing children! The blessings around my first marriage are my three amazing children. I love being a mom! My children show me how strong love can be! I love them so much I would move mountains for them!

Lyle and I continued to grow further apart and after 18 years of marriage to Lyle , our marriage ended in divorce.

I thought all would be fine since I was divorced from Lyle. However, my mind went to a place of victimization. I began searching for help because I wanted to know and live as being victorious in Christ. Searching for help, I turned to a pastor of a church we were visiting at the time. The pastor told me he didn't agree with divorce and he didn't know what to do with divorced people.

I searched and found out about DivorceCare at a church close to where I lived. DivorceCare is a divorce recovery support group led by godly leaders where you can find help and healing for the hurt of divorce. After each class, I began to see I was not wearing a big letter "D" for divorced for the world to not know what to do with me. It was nice to be accepted, even in my hurt. At this church, they did seem to know what to do with divorced people. They loved me the way Jesus loves, yes, even in the mud and mire of my crushed self. They invited me to fellowship events. I attended some of the events and felt more and more valued. I later joined this church, the one that took me in when I was hurting the most and loved me through it all.

Through the guidance of the Holy Spirit, counseling, and my pastors, I learned that God desires a relationship with each one of us. I realized God is too big to be kept in my "as needed box." The more I prayed and became closer to God, the more I began to know peace. I discovered it was all right to open up and share my feelings with people I trusted. Mostly, I learned to share my thoughts and feelings with God. After all, God knew them anyway!

During the eighteen years of marriage to Lyle, I turned to a comfort I had turned to years ago. The comfort of eating. As my weight increased, I felt even more worthless. I would drive through fast food places, and if one supersize meal was good, then two meals would be even better. I would tell myself, "Just throw all this food out the window" as I drove away, knowing I was hurting myself. However, it smelled and tasted so good, and I thought, "The next time, I will do better." I would find a place to eat in secret by myself. Feeding the insecurities within myself was causing more insecurities. Like an endless cycle, I would enjoy eating food that was making me feel awful, ashamed, and guilty. This caused an endless cycle of completely being out of balance. As I ate and made unhealthy food choices, the number on the scale grew. I disliked myself more and more. I think the weight served to bury my sadness more and more, so I believed.

Shortly after living as a single mom, I was tucking my daughter into bed in our new house that God had helped us find by way of a rainbow. We had been praying over this home while living with my parents, and one day, after raining, there was a beautiful rainbow in the sky that ended right at the road our house was on. My daughter was the one who saw the rainbow. Days later, the price dropped on the house at a level I could afford, and the house became ours. What a joy that my daughter, who years before at the young age of four had told me "Mommy, you are all bound up, but about to be set free" was now seeing rainbows.

After reading her favorite book and saying prayers, my daughter looked me in my eyes with the covers warmly pulled up close to her and said, "Mommy, I am so glad we have our house and we have peace!" I tucked the covers around her, gave her a sweet kiss goodnight on her forehead, and responded, "Me too sweetheart, me too."

Years after my divorce, I traveled to the beach and spent some time sitting by the ocean. This was when God revealed an amazing vision as I looked into the vast, deep, dark blue water. This vision brought me hope that spread light into some deep, dark places of pain from my past.

I was looking for the shore of assurance; however, I could not see past the waves of my past. I started to discover that I was looking for circumstances or met dreams to complete me. I was looking for something, an event, or anyone else to give me purpose. After I saw the vision, which I will go into detail about in the following pages, I discovered my past pain could have a voice of hope and that I would get to unravel layers within myself to begin a much desired transformation. The transformation began with me and God, with God leading the path, of course. I prayed, "God, be my mirror. Let me see with the lens that you want me to look through, and that includes looking through the lens of God to see within myself."

The vision that I saw during my walk along the ocean that day caused me to stop in amazement! I saw all the waves in the ocean in twos! Even the birds flying over the ocean were in twos! The waves of twos almost frightened me! I rubbed my eyes and blinked and looked again. Again, all the waves were paired, two waves growing higher, two separate waves farther out in the ocean coming to shore. As far as I could see, there were waves paired in twos, even the waves that were coming to shore! Even the little waves that, yes, even as an adult, I still liked jumping over like when I was little at the beach with my dad.

The Holy Spirit spoke to me in my spirit during my vision, not an audible voice, but a hope filled my spirit of, "Two by two, I am here for you, my beautiful child." "Lean on me, and know you are never alone." "I am here for you always, in times of valleys and times on top of the mountain soaring." "Your wings will heal and you will fly again with hope. You will soar on eagles' wings! You are not alone." I was amazed that the God of the entire universe cared enough to send me this vision at exactly the perfect timing when He knew my eyes and ears would be open to see and hear Him !

This vision opened an awareness of light that began to shine into dark areas of my past. I desired to know more about my Savior who cares for me and is on this journey with me. I sensed I was not alone, and I was paired with Jesus, two by two, us two, Jesus and me! I desired to grow closer to Jesus and learn more about him!

I began surrendering my life to God to transform me to a better me, not a perfect me, but a me that God created me to be. I exclaimed to myself, "No wonder you have been out of balance. You have been pretending to be someone other than God made you to be, Debra!" I was trying to please others instead of God! I opened the box I was keeping God in all those years, and in setting Him free from His box, He began to set me free from the chains I was wrapped in!

Through turning to pray more, I began to open my eyes to desiring to remove the veil of victimization and accept the victory found in Jesus Christ to overcome obstacles in my way.

I began to hold onto God's constant unchanging love and hope found in Jesus Christ, my Savior. I began to feel accepted and loved for who I was for the first time! I was falling in love with Jesus! Past ashes were on a journey becoming redeemed with only beauty to behold! The chain links of untrue beliefs about myself started to shake around my soul and break!

I began a path of renewing my mind, body, and spirit. I continued to pray faithfully to God, and felt the Holy Spirit lead me to start exercising and adapt to a healthier lifestyle.

Once I returned home from my weekend at the beach as a new single mom, I walked into the gym, wondering if I would be laughed at, being very overweight. The opposite happened. People were nice and encouraging. One of the trainers smiled as I was leaving after walking on the treadmill and said, "See you tomorrow, Debra." It felt good to not be judged. I saw a picture of the trainer on the bulletin board and read his story of transformation from unhealthy choices to healthy choices.

The only one judging me as I walked into the gym that day was me judging myself. I was still holding on to a link of that chain of striving for the perfect number on a scale completing me, even though God had snapped those chains free.

Transformation is a process that involves renewing my mind daily, staying in the truth of God's word, and repeating the process each day.

Encouragement from true friends you trust helps as well. Friends who want the best for you are an amazing gift from God. One of my friends encouraged me to not give up as I began making healthier lifestyle changes by exercising and choosing food choices I carefully thought about. I would ask myself, most of the times I ate, if I thought God felt this food was good for me.

As I started healing on the inside, I began to eat healthier and continue to go to the gym, and I lost 132 pounds!! I began to gain attention from men.

Years after my divorce, I dated a great guy named Chase. He had a heart of gold. He raced at a local racetrack, and I felt like a teenager cheering him on as he drove his car around the track! I even helped him and his crew in the racing "pits"! We quickly learned we were better as friends. Chase later passed away from cancer.

I did not date much, as I was very cautious of dating, and I had a wall around my heart that was made of strong iron. I knew I had healing to do, and I wanted to be healed from my divorce before I became close to someone else. So, I continued to dream and desire that maybe one day, God would send the one He picked out for my life. I never asked God through prayer anything about Lyle before I married him, so I thought this time, I will ask God to write my love story!

I believed once the pounds dropped off the scale, I would be balanced in my mind as well. However, I was still out of balance.

Instead of food, the scale now made me feel better. If the number on the scale "said" I was at a "good" weight, I felt great! My feelings were elevated! If the scale "said" an increase or "bad" weight, I would feel low.

Where was the balance in my life? If the number on the scale had increased, I would exercise and then weigh myself five to seven times a day, hoping the results would change. No matter the results, in my mind, I was always overweight. What a burden to carry in my mind.

I was looking for balance in the wrong places. I was so sure when I saw the vision along the ocean that I would always know my definition was being a child of God and that would be enough. However, here I was looking for balance somewhere else besides God. I was looking at a number on a scale and even giving it a voice in my definition!

The definition of balance[15] as a noun is "an even distribution of weight enabling someone to remain upright and steady." As a verb, balance is defined as "to keep or put something in a steady position so that it does not fall."

When I think of balance, I think of a seesaw. I actually wondered if my life was but a seesaw. I noted that in the past, when my seesaw was very low, I would overcompensate with the wrong things to try to get my seesaw back in balance. I would overeat, overspend, overreact, overanalyze, and overcling to unhealthy relationships with a few of the guys I dated. Sounds like my "overs and unders" that I mentioned in earlier pages had reappeared to show their ugly selves!

My joy, at times, was attached to a level of an attainment of a goal based in my mind, such as a perfect weight, a perfect man, or a perfect response. If I felt any goal was not being met, I would sometimes find a quick "exit ramp" to a new pathway. This "exit ramp" was simply looking for a new "new" to fulfill me.

My brain had learned escape routes while living in hurtful situations in my past. It was time for my brain to learn some

---

15 See footnotes.

new pathways not linked to hurt I had expected in the past. I had to learn that my life was more than living in survival mode.

I was reminded of the vision God had shown me in that "WOW moment" on the beach. I know if I lean on the unending hope found in Jesus, I will not need to search for an "exit" ramp. In the hope of Jesus, my true contentment of who I am will be found. Jesus is my new pathway. It is small footsteps at a time, not giant leaps. I still occasionally slip back into grasping another chain link of untrue beliefs. Thankfully, the closer I lean on God, the quicker He brings me back to His truth.

We are created for a relationship with the One who created us. When you, the created, spend more time with God, your creator, you become more comfortable. You begin to know more about your creator and you start to know you, the created, even better.

In the bible I am reminded God never leaves or forsakes us.[16] Even though my life was out of balance, God was still at the center core of me.

I am thankful for good friends who have stood by my side through the years. One weekend, a friend and her husband invited me on a weekend adventure of fishing the New River.

I met them there at the two-story house we reserved. I invited one of my friends along. We started our day of fishing, and I did not catch many fish, but I loved being outside. After fishing all day, we had plans to spend time by the campfire roasting marshmallows.

---

16 NIV, See footnotes.

After fishing at the New River, we returned to the house to prepare for our campfire. My jeans, longer than they should have been, were wet from fishing in the river. I took my shoes off, and my baggy, long jeans hung over my feet. Being excited about the evening plans and anxious to get the campfire started, I did not take the time to attend to my jean hem. I hurriedly started downstairs. My right big toe got under the hem of my jeans, and I tripped at the top of the stairs headfirst!

I suffered a fall from a flight of stairs, tumbling head over heels! Unlike all the fish I had missed earlier, my fleeing body did not miss hitting each and every step!

During the fall from the top of the stairs, I felt my neck hit one of the concrete steps and I became unconscious after that. There was an accordion-style door opening at the bottom of the concrete steps that was always only half-open. It was not open enough for someone to fit through most of the time.

After my "try at gymnastic tumbling" where you could say I did not win a medal, I awoke at the bottom of the stairs sitting straight up! Yes! I fell asleep during the fall and woke up sitting straight up, with a feeling of peace! I believe, without a doubt, God took a hold of me and softly, gently sat me up at the bottom of those stairs! God's ways are mysterious for sure, even through an accordion-style door!

My friends came to check on me and asked if I was all right. In my stubbornness, I told them, "Yes, I am fine." I got up, and the pain in my upper neck area was intense. I walked up to the top of the stairs and knew something was not right. Grabbing the mask of pretending I had worn in the past and not wanting to spoil the plans of the campfire, I pretended I was all right.

I quietly walked down the hallway to the back room of the house and called my doctor. My doctor told me to lie down immediately and call 911! Being the nurse I am, I told him, "I think I am fine, and I don't see a need to call 911." He insisted, thank God.

I walked down the hall from the bedroom and into the kitchen where my friends were gathering food to cook over the fire. I told my friends, "Please keep cooking, and you all enjoy the campfire. I don't know why, but my doctor has asked me to lie down on the couch and call 911, so the paramedics are coming shortly!" Of course, my friends stopped cooking and sat with me until the paramedics arrived.

"I honestly don't know why I am doing this. I'm sure the pain will improve if I give it time," I told the paramedics when they arrived.

The paramedics placed me in a neck brace and carefully transported me to the hospital in West Jefferson, North Carolina. My friends drove behind the ambulance. The emergency room doctor ordered a scan. After listening to the loud sound of the scanning machine, I went from wondering how those campfire roasted marshmallows would be tasting about now to wondering if I was a piece of laundry in a large washing machine. After the "rinse cycle," I was wheeled on my stretcher back to my room in the emergency department to wait on the results. I imagined being discharged soon so I could return to the house to roast marshmallows and hot dogs by the fire!

Shortly, a young handsome doctor, Dr. Ross, opened the door to my room and said calmly, "Ms. Debra, we need to transfer you immediately to the nearest trauma center. You have broken your neck." "What?! This can't be. I am a single mom of three! I don't have anyone to help me. I can't have broken my neck," I said in disbelief. I asked Dr. Ross, "Am I going to be paralyzed?" Dr. Ross responded, "Possibly, but it is a good sign so far you can move your extremities." Now, shattered, broken bones to add to my journey.

As I laid on the stretcher, awaiting the ambulance ride to the trauma center, I felt God blanket me with His presence. Jeremiah 29:11-14[17] says, "For I know the plans I have for you," declares the Lord, "plans to prosper you and not to harm you, plans to give you hope and a future. Then you will call on me and come and pray to me, and I will listen to you. You will seek me and find me when you seek me with all your heart. I will be found by you," declares the Lord "and will bring you back from captivity." (NIV)

This scripture from Jeremiah covered my spirit, this single mom of three. The comfort of God not only blanketed me, God balanced me. God took this time as a great opportunity to heal me from the inside out. I took advantage of this time to draw closer to God. I had to rely on others, as I was in a neck brace for three months. I guess since I was in a neck brace, God knew I was only able to look forward! We are never alone, and God comforts us!

God took a hold of me on that stairwell and softly placed me in a sitting position. He covered me in His love! God took a hold of me during the fall and saved my life and continued to give me the gift of walking and breathing.

After I was transferred to the trauma center, Dr. Goodwin performed a neurological exam and was concerned about one

17 NIV, See footnotes.

of the tests. He repeated the test and then said, "You worried me for a minute, but you are fine." "It looks like if your spine stays in alignment, you may not need surgery. We will refer you to a spine specialist, who will keep a good watch on your spine alignment." I insisted on doing as much as I could there at the trauma center, telling Dr. Goodwin I was so thankful for each step and breath. I told him I wanted to do as much as I could on my own. Dr. Goodwin said, "Amen, the Good Lord was watching over you, Debra. If the break had been higher up or lower, the effect of the fall could have been totally different. You could have stopped breathing or been paralyzed from the neck down."

I thanked Dr. Goodwin, called my family, and was driven home, me and my neck brace buddy for three months. Amazingly, God gave me amazing rest each night and time to heal from the inside out.

Isaiah 41:13 tells us, "For I am the Lord your God who takes hold of your right hand and says to you, Do not fear; I will help you"[18] Thanks be to God.

After this time of healing from the inside out, I came to a place in my life where I was ready to take off the mask I would sometimes pick up and wear. I did not want to choose a mask to match the cause and effect seasons and determinants of my life. I was tired of telling myself I was defined by a number on a scale, or a guy who would show me attention, or any met or unmet goal checked off my list.

Proverbs 11:1 says "A false balance is abomination to the Lord: but a just weight is His delight."[19] (KJV) I was tired of

---

18 NIV, See footnotes.
19 KJV, See footnotes.

waiting for some guy to complete my life or the perfect circumstance. I learned if I looked to another person to keep me balanced, I was in for my seesaw hitting ground zero!! When I look to God to be my core, my center, I feel balanced. I find peace that is beyond understanding by leaning on God.

Matthew 6:33 reminds us, "But seek first His kingdom and His righteousness, and all these things will be given to you as well."[20]

After my neck healed, I hiked in the mountains one day. As my heart began to heal, I began seeing God's beauty deeper! I saw a waterfall along one of the trails, and I stopped to watch how freely the water poured over the rocks. I began to cry. "So, that is what a waterfall looks like," I said to myself. I felt the blinders over my eyes were being removed one by one. I envisioned Band-Aids on my heart being healed one by one, one section at a time.

God led me to many beautiful ministries at my church to keep healing my heart and to set my mind on a pathway to healing from victimization to victory in Jesus. I was hoping I would not pull the scab of healing off to start all over, as I had done in the past. One of these ministries was Celebrate Recovery, a ministry for anyone who is hurting, has hang-ups, or has unhealthy habits. I thought, I have hurts, habits, and hang ups, so this sounded like a place for me. I also desired to know how God could help me remove my pretending mask and truly know how to be victorious through Christ, so I decided to attend one evening of Celebrate Recovery at my church.

---

20 NIV, See footnotes.

Any new situation can be scary for me. I drove to the church, parked my car, and walked in with my weak knees shaking. They had a meal first. I was greeted by such nice people, and I felt welcomed there.

After eating, I walked to the worship center and enjoyed worshipping God. The band was amazing! After worship, I attended an orientation session about Celebrate Recovery, letting me know what to expect for the small groups I would attend the next week. The nice, kind minister there told me to give it three weeks and see what I thought. After the orientation session for the new visitors, we gathered for snacks. I felt I belonged among others who were seeking to grow with Jesus right through their hurts, habits, and hang-ups.

I attended the next week, and after worship, attended my first small group with other ladies. I liked that the group shared small group guidelines. The guidelines made me feel safe that no one there would judge me, talk over me, or try to fix me. The group facilitator, with such kind eyes, shared that Celebrate Recovery is a Christ-centered recovery ministry. I liked the way that sounded. I learned so much from the lessons, the testimonies, and the group sessions. It was here I learned what codependency was, and I could see this throughout my life. I attended a Step Study where I learned to examine the layers of my life and to balance the positives with the things I could improve in my life. I was never judged. My relationship with Jesus grew deeper by attending Celebrate Recovery.

I learned more about accountability and how important it is to have someone you trust to walk alongside you. This shy girl, after attending many months with the strength of God, stood at the tall podium and shared her story one evening!

Soon after, I was blessed to be a facilitator of the post-traumatic stress group for women and the women's "A to Z group." God led each group, and I was blessed by each child of God there.

Being nervous at first about volunteering, and knowing I was not able without God, I told myself, "Just show up, Debra. God will do the rest." God always comes through just in time.

Many years later after my divorce and on my road to growing deeper in love with Jesus, mutual friends introduced me to a handsome country boy named Roary ("Moe") who loved to hunt.

We started dating, and I began to see hearts everywhere! I saw leaves in the shape of hearts, heart shapes in the sand along seashores, hearts everywhere throughout my days, hearts while hiking, and even hearts from a huge buck while hunting one day with Moe. I felt so safe and so loved next to Moe. I loved how he protected me. I felt our hearts melt into one when he hugged me! I was in love, and that love leaped out of my heart and soul into his strong arms each time I saw him!

After dating over three years, this handsome country boy with the eyes that spoke to my soul got on one knee after a day of hunting and asked me to marry him!! I quickly said, "Yes!!" God had written our love story, and what a lot of love revealed!! We had a wedding of my dreams September 12, 2015, and on that day, all my sight was on my husband.

The wonderment of God sending me my love added a question to our love story shortly after a year of being married. The question of "Why, God, Why?" when my husband was given the diagnosis of esophageal cancer due to Barrett's esophagus. Words like chemo, port-a-cath, numbers, and clinical trials now entered our newlywed lives. When I heard the word cancer, I went numb. Our life of dreams shattered in my mind, and the old coping skills tried to creep into my mind and take over. I felt I was drowning! My husband, speaking strength, said to me, "Honey, you always say to trust God. We get to trust God in this."

I just cannot put into words the pain in my heart. I literally felt my heart ache. When I would see my husband's struggle to eat on his toughest days, my heart would melt with tears. The tears that flowed down my cheek tasted like the salt in the ocean! I would hide to eat or drink because I felt I should struggle to eat or drink as well. My husband would say, "Honey, come eat here beside me." "God, please just take this cancer from my husband and give it to me," I would cry out in my inner self, trying to remain strong as his wife, his helpmate.

I would recall moments where God would remind me of struggles through my past hurts, broken bones, brokenness, divorce, and many valleys of lies and uncertainty. God would remind me of whispers of "I love you," steadiness, balance, and honesty. I believe this kept me upright, along with the amazing strength of my husband. If I had not been through hurt before, would I have the strength now? I had seen the work of God in healing, so I expected healing for my husband.

My husband desired to live life as normal and not let cancer take over our lives. We still went hunting and spent much time together, still believing we would grow old together and accomplish our dreams. We planned to build a beautiful house together and loved dreaming of what was to be discovered in our years to come. I saw even more hearts day to day in abundance, as if God was sending love notes along this new journey called cancer.

This journey had bouts of depression at times for me, along with anxiety, feelings of drowning, and yes, anger at God for "allowing this to happen." When well-meaning people would say "I'm sorry," triggers would ignite inside me that seemed to take me to that cleft with my name on it I had visited in my past. I felt if I hid in the cleft of the rock, I could slow life down and peek out and prepare to enter slowly back into the world at my own pace of safety where others seemed to be just living and moving right along.

One minute, I was singing praises in the storm, feeling God's presence, and the next minute, I was taking shelter in my aloofness away from a perceived tornado. I'm running!; I'm drowning!; I'm clinging!; I'm screaming on the inside!; I'm gentle; I'm kind; I'm loving, all within a matter of minutes.

I was, at times, angry with those who have "perfect" lives who seem to be worried about a paper clip not matching their paper color or worried about their clothes matching. All the while, I was feeling good to have had energy to get dressed that day among my fear of that cancer.

When cancer came into our lives, I am not proud to say that I felt I was being punished for not being a "good enough" Christian. Little things would trigger my feelings of fear of the unknown. Oddly enough, during this time, people that spoke about their "perfect" lives triggered past feelings within me of escape modes that were buried inside me.

Once, I attended a covered dish meal at a community event where it took all the energy I had to go purchase a dessert and attend. When I arrived, I carried my dessert and placed it on the food table. The ladies who seemed to be "in charge of the food table" approached the table quickly, and my dessert was quickly looked at, taken off the table, and whisked away to the kitchen. I thought they must not need any more desserts, and then I quickly saw all the other desserts were homemade and showcased. Now, I know it sounds funny to say my feelings were hurt over a dessert.

I was so proud that I even mustered up the energy to attend a place I thought I would have good fellowship. Instead, my store-bought dessert was demoted to the kitchen where it stayed. I felt I was placed at the "don't talk to her table, she brought store-bought dessert." I know, I think it sounds silly to me now too that I felt that way.

I sat and listened while the ladies shared their recipe stories for their showcased ribbon-winning homemade desserts and giggled how they had to hide their baked goods from their husbands after they baked. Tears welled up in my eyes. I wish my husband had his appetite and could eat like he used to. My husband would have been happy with my store-bought dessert.

I left my store-bought dessert in the kitchen when the luncheon was over, quickly walked to my car, and cried. During the fight of cancer, even demoted store-bought desserts can make you cry. The luncheon was certainly not about someone eating my store-bought dessert and it was not about me. It did surprise me at the "triggers" to my hurts or my "used to be" that surfaced.

To be fair, the ladies there did not know what my heart was going through, and if I had opened up, I am sure I would have been included in the conversation. Triggers to our deep hurts can surface at any time, just like a washed-up seashell can wash up to our feet along the ocean. That seashell, I am sure, journeyed through many sights before it was broken or washed up on the shore. The seashell was probably much deeper, and then it was brought to the surface, even in its brokenness. It seemed like during our journey of cancer and often if I had a lack of sleep, the triggers that would bring tears could be the tiniest, most incidental occurrences. I saw many hurts come to the surface at times I never would have expected them to surface again. I learned that healing is not always a "check that off and move on approach." Sometimes, old familiar ways try to demand attention again.

Remember the white pelican that my friend Bea told me about? I imagine I looked like a white pelican at the luncheon that day, retreating myself to the "don't talk to me "table. I imagine white pelicans are frustrated with the other birds around them, like I was frustrated with the ladies at the luncheon.

In the Bible, there are many stories of times people were ready to give up. Elijah was one who became frustrated with God's people and was ready to give up. God pursued him anyway.

God knows everything about us, like he knew Elijah was worn out. He knows when we are as well. God is with us through our storms of life. We most often find answers in the still, small voice telling us to reach out to those who show love and are accepting of us, walking alongside us right where we are. We get to share with those we trust and accept the gift of someone walking with us right where we are. Even during the calamities in our lives, stop and listen for the still, small voice of God. God is with us always.

During Valentine's Day weekend of 2017, eight months into our cancer journey, my husband said to me, "Honey, let's go to the beach." We journeyed there and we fished a lot. It was there Moe shared with me, "Honey, I wish I could feel like I did when I was young."

God led me back to journaling there on the seashore. Journaling was not new to me. I started journaling many years ago, and found it fascinating to see how God moves. I thought I would remember my prayers through the years; however, I have found journaling helps me to remember ones that probably would have been buried into forgetfulness. I find it fascinating and reassuring to see I am not where I used to be on this journey called life. Journaling has shown me God's truth, along with turning to the Bible, our guide map for life.

God awoke me each morning to see the sunrise at the beach. As mentioned in the introduction, I noticed the birds were not moving and were very still, on the shore, until the sun arose. Then, the birds all began their flight. It was so beautiful! It was as if the birds danced as the sun arose for the new day! It made me more aware of the gift of a wonderful loving Son who arose also! So, hence the name of the book you are reading now, *And The Birds Danced*. **Author's Note:** *The picture on the cover was taken by myself on Valentine's weekend 2017. I was able to capture a glimpse of God's amazing creation during the sunrise as well as one of the many birds that took flight on that beautiful morning, along the shore.*

That weekend at the beach was full of God moments for me and my husband. We felt God's presence all around us! We felt hope, and we truly believed God would throw my husband's cancer in the depths of the sea! In years past, within the old me, news such as that cancer would tempt me to grab chains of past insecurities and false beliefs. However, now I know a new way to cope that involves turning to Jesus.

No chains of past hurts, no chains of cancer, and no chains of fears or unknowns hold me!! I am a child of God. I get to take hold of Jesus, and I know He walks alongside me. Jesus is greater than any circumstances! I know God is with me even on side roads or whether I am soaring like an eagle or when I am face down flat on my face crying out to God or whether I am walking on solid ground, hard pavement roads, or steady, soft sand ahead. God is with me!

The hurt in the past which explains what my daughter saw in my eyes years ago was well on its way to healing; however, I was keenly aware of this new journey of cancer and its fiery darts and the damage it could do!

Cancer, love, fear, hope, doubt, trust, and faith. Like the kids show when I was little would say, "Which of these words is not like the others? Which words do not belong in the grouping cancer, love, fear, hope, doubt, trust, and faith?" Of course, "The words cancer, fear, and doubt do not belong," I tell myself.

However, God showed me, even in seasons of storms and during deep wounds in my life, there is hope! Yes hope, along with love, trust, and faith. Those all fit right along with whatever storm or shattered dream you may be experiencing. How would we even get through the storm if hope, love, faith, and trust were not paired with the storm?

Like the vision I saw years earlier of each wave being in pairs, storms are paired with hope, love, faith, and trust. Name your companions to your storm or hurt. Before you turn to an addiction or an idol, like I turned to lies in my mind, food, or the scale for example, it is a good idea to look beyond the wave and reach toward the shoreline for accountability and help on your journey. If you have picked up anyone or anything to heal your hurts without looking to Jesus, I encourage you to turn to Jesus for help. Finding a godly link to pair with your storm or hurt is a great discovery to begin your journey of transformation. Stoop down, pick up the shattered pieces of your storm, cup them in your hand covered with God's love and hope, and move faithfully forward.

Being a newlywed after marrying Moe, I was finally content at being closer to the true me I had hid from years earlier. Being a newlywed is not what made me content and at peace, although I always thought being a wife to the man of my dreams would complete me. What made me content and at peace was my awareness and growth with my relationship with Jesus all those years before I met Moe. I found that another person, a dream, an accomplishment, or a goal I had set for myself would not complete me. I found that Jesus is my path to healing, peace, and contentment!

My daughters and others finally saw hope, freedom, and peace in my eyes! Peace! I felt peace finally, even though I did not know what tomorrow would bring.

Hope! I feel hope at this moment, even though I do not know what tomorrow brings or which way the crossroads will go.

God! I feel God's presence, even though I do not know what tomorrow will bring or which roads are ahead.

I often revisit thoughts of that Valentine's weekend at the beach in 2017. My husband loved to fish as well as hunt. When I caught fish, it was my husband who taught me how to take the fish off the line. It was my husband who was so patient with me on days on the lake that I honestly caught more tree limbs than fish! When I would catch a catfish, my husband would reach over to take the catfish off the line to protect me from the sting.

Thinking back to that Valentine's weekend and remembering me and Moe sharing that beautiful sunny day together, I remember my husband wanted to go fishing. I knew my husband was having one of his rough days in the cancer fight; however, he never complained. He taught me what strength looked like. I learned so much from him on how to face adversity with strength, love, faith, and trust in God. So, we grabbed our fishing gear and we journeyed to the pier.

Journal Entries, Scriptures, and Inspirations

"We now have this light shining in our hearts, but we ourselves are like fragile clay jars containing this great treasure. This makes it clear that our great power is from God, not from ourselves." 2 Corinthians 4:7 (NLT)[21]

"The tears He has allowed to dim the eyes
of my flesh have cleared the eyes of my soul, bringing
each time a new depth of spiritual understanding and
vision because I trust Him. The woman at the well loves
Christ with her whole heart and she is not ashamed to tell
the world what He has done for her"[22]
—DALE EVANS

God revealed life;
God revealed hearts;
God revealed hope;
God revealed restoration.

---

21 NLT, See footnotes.
22 See footnotes.

Notes: How This Applies:

Take The Next Step Idea: Write your story:

Next Step Idea:

Has anyone ever given you a second chance?

Has anyone ever shown you grace and/or mercy?

Have you ever shown grace and/or mercy to someone else?

Consider thinking or writing about these times.

Chapter 3

Trusting Even When
I Don't See

We reached our destination with fishing poles in hand! We fished on the pier and even caught a shark! Full of excitement for the next catch, we ventured to the shore, dreaming to catch lots of fish! I learned fishing against the waves is not for beginners like me, but I enjoyed trying!

We sat on the shore until that beautiful sunrise I had seen glowing brightly into the sky that morning turned to moonlight that would guide our path back to our oceanside room. However, we were not ready to take the path back to our room yet. As that night progressed on the seashore, we were sitting with our fishing poles. I was feeling my husband's heart beating as we held hands, clenched together as one. I savored the moment.

I recorded his voice on my phone, as if I was asking God to help me remember that moment. I desired for time to stop right then along the shore and that I would always remember the sound of his voice, the strength of his arms, and the safety and protection I felt being with him.

The look of pure unconditional love in Moe's eyes when he looked into my eyes spoke to my soul. The crashing waves of the ocean as we sat on the shore was not something I was hearing or seeing at that time. My eyes were focused on my love! It reminded me of our wedding day when I only saw my husband! I may not have heard the ocean waves that night; however, each wave spoke to my spirit.

I asked myself, "Lord, am I meant to hold onto blessings, or are blessings, like feathers in flight, for me to only behold for just a moment?"

Why does my husband, the kindest, most loving, most humble, and strongest man I know have cancer?

"God, I know you are able to remove this cancer and throw it in the depths of the sea! Please Lord, answer my prayer and heal my husband's cancer. Please God, I plead! I cry out within myself."

You see, as a child, I learned to wait for endings. My best friend would move away, my grandparents' deaths, my true self dying each day as I felt so strangely different than others, miscarriage, broken bones, and broken hearts. "Please Lord," I cried, "please do not end this most wonderful gift of my husband I prayed for and treasure so!"

Beginning to be too concerned about my past, my mind slowed down and my focus waivered away from my mind to the shore.

As we sat on the shore in the glowing moonlight, I saw a seashell in three pieces. I beheld its beauty. Even among my fears inside and my silent questions to God within myself, I saw beauty and signs of hope all around me. I thought to my-self, "Enjoy this moment. Enjoy the present time. Each second is a gift."

We sat as two along the shore, our fishing lines in the ocean, forgetting we were waiting to catch fish. Moe saw the red light on my phone light up in the moonlight and he asked, "Honey, are you recording my voice?" We smiled, we laughed, and he said, "I love you, Honey, you are my best catch ever." I said with a smile, "I am glad you did not throw me back, Honey." Then, I said, "Yes, Honey, I am recording your voice. I love you too, Honey."

I whispered a prayer to God, asking God for my husband to stay there with me forever. Again, I asked that the cancer in his body would be thrown into the deep sea that sat in front of us!

I felt another's presence with us along the shore, the same presence I felt each time we walked hand in hand down the long glass hallway at the cancer center. God is always with us, right alongside us. Three cords cannot be broken. God is with us, no matter where we travel!

Not catching many fish, we gathered our fishing rods and tackle and began our walk back to our room.

Walking across the soft sand with the birds anxiously watching our every move, as if they were hoping we would share our leftover bait from fishing, my husband squeezed my hand.

As his body inside was fighting cancer, he looked tired. He said, "Honey, I just want to feel young again." I clenched his hand tighter and I whispered, "I know, Honey. I know."

Sometimes, we discover paths to beginnings of trusting in God when we admit to God we fear endings.

Journal Entries, Scriptures, and Inspirations

And the birds danced, heartbeat in hands, clenched together as one. Under the stars, I smell the salt water in the air as I ask God to help me remember. Tears add to the salt air falling into the waves. Some waves calm, others with force with ebb and flow. My heart is broken. In the brokenness, what must it take for me to hear God's voice? Are my ears open without the broken? Oh, to hear His voice in all. Take my broken and spread like rays of light from sunrise. Once sunrise presents for day, the birds dance and soar, for the moment, the present moment presents itself. Treasured heartbeat in hand, and so, the birds dance in God's light.

Written by the seashore Valentine's Day 2017.

Author's note: *The heartbeats in hand refers to me feeling my husband's heartbeat when he held my hand. To me, this represents hope. Hope, much in the same way birds take flight as the sun rises each new day. I would ask God to help me remember each time I felt this precious heartbeat in my hand, that I may never forget.*

Isaiah 40:31 "But they that wait upon the Lord shall renew their strength; they shall mount up with wings as eagles;

they shall run, and not be weary; and they shall walk, and not faint." KJV[23]

"Getting over a painful experience is much like crossing monkey bars. You have to let go at some point in order to move forward."[24]
—C.S. Lewis

"Let God have your life; He can do more with it than you can."[25]
—Dwight L. Moody

Proverbs 4:25-26 "Let your eyes look straight ahead; fix your gaze directly before you. Give careful thought to the paths for your feet and be steadfast in all your ways." (NIV)[26]

Proverbs 3:5 "Trust in the Lord with all your heart and lean not on your own understanding." (NIV)[27]

Psalm 62:8 "Trust in him at all times, you people; pour out your hearts to him, for God is our refuge." (NIV)[28]

---

23 KJV, See footnotes.
24 See footnotes.
25 See footnotes.
26 NIV, See footnotes.
27 NIV, See footnotes.
28 NIV, See footnotes.

"The Three Birds and The Branch"

Walked with Jesus today;
Saw three birds: a cardinal, a bluebird, and a robin.
The precious birds, all three, fly for a moment, land,
and are still among the steady branch.

At this moment in time,
the cardinal catches my eye particularly.
My thoughts move to the branch
going through its own seasons;
For both will never be the same.

All changed by the flight and the landing.

The bird is being watched over in flight
as its wings fly among it all and through it all.
The strong steady branch,
not swaying here nor there, not bending from the wind;
As if the branch awaits what God's calling has in store.

God is steadfast and true.
A steady branch accepts the beautiful bird just as it is.
The bird is provided for during
each season of the flight and landing.

Thanks be to God, Our Father, Son,
Jesus Christ, and Holy Spirit; three in one.

Thankful for the three birds and the strong steady branch.

Thankful for the flight and the landing.

God is with us as we venture out on a limb onto the branch
and as we take flight again;
We get to trust Him, our provider.

Jehovah-Jireh: The Lord will provide.

Trust is defined as "a firm belief in the reliability, truth, ability,
or strength of someone. [29]

---

29 See footnotes.

Notes/How This Applies:

Take The Next Step Ideas: Think about or write about where you put your trust.

Think of a truth you know for sure:

Name two abilities God has gifted you with:

Do you ever wish to be taken back to a season in your life? If so, would you go back?

If you are plowing a field, can you plow looking backward? Can you take a season of growth and plant it in your life, water it, and expectantly hope it will sprout up, especially when a storm appears?

Will that season of growth continue to grow if we don't water it? Imagine watering your growing season and imagine the growing season sprouting up life to nourish you during seasons of drought, storms, or shattered dreams.

Feel free to take some time and ponder these things and journal your thoughts on your note pages.

Often, when I call out to God, it brings comfort and peace. I found it amazing to look at letters from the past and see how God answered prayers. God may answer, "Not now, maybe later, or yes." Often, just talking with God gives me a feeling of not being alone. Sharing and relying on God gives me hope.

I would like to share some of the actual letters when I wrote to God or cried out to God. They include seasons of thankfulness, pouring out desires of my heart, and some to worship God. Hidden treasures can surely be revealed in letters! I often remind myself to slow down and stop and listen to the guidance of the Holy Spirit who lives inside of me.

My friend Lylia regularly plans a date night with God. She plans and sets the most beautiful table with fresh flowers and a meal she has lovingly prepared. She prepares the finest china and the finest linens and sets a table for two. One for Jesus and one for herself. She told me that her date with Jesus is her finest date ever!

I envisioned myself setting up and inviting Jesus for a date night as well. I set the finest table, cleaned, and prepared the finest meal I could . Even in the preparation, my heart felt joy. I gave Jesus the chair at the head of the table. I felt my Savior loving me more than ever. I quieted my spirit from the "why, God, why?" to "thank you, God for walking alongside me." I learned to envision more than my circumstances. I learned to envision, in a stronger way, God's love for us. It is so big and vast, I truly can only imagine it!

Envision, envision, envision! In the next chapter are some of my letters to God.

Chapter 4

Letters to God

Dear God,
Thank you for angels. I am trying to pray faithfully. Remind me, God every day, every minute that you are all I will ever need.

I pray for patience, dear God. I trust in Your plan. I am so thankful for you, and I desire to know you more, Lord. Move my heart!

I thank you, God for freedom. Dear God, I often remember your words that came through my beautiful daughter, as a child, when she looked into my eyes and said, as if her words came from you (which I believe they were), "You have been all bound up, but you are about to be set free!"

Your promises are true, Lord. Thank you, God so very much for releasing my chains.

Dear God, my rescuer, help me to spend more time right now learning to walk again in my faith journey.

Help my eagle wings rest for now, and I pray my wings you have given me will someday be ready for flight and will soar from the mountaintop proclaiming Your word, Your will always.

Love, Debra

Dear God,

I wish to remember all you have done for me so I could say thank you. Please be patient with me, Lord. My memory isn't very good. I have been too busy and concerned about my own life to notice Your life in me. But it's coming back to me, little by little. Bear with me and help me through your Holy Spirit. I choose to meditate upon all your works and consider all your mighty deeds, all of them. Because the more I remember you, the more I feel loved. The more I am loved, the more I can love. As my memory grows, so does my gratitude. As more gratitude grows, so does my desire to love you with my entire heart. Thank you, Lord, for everything.

Love, Debra

Lord, I can't do this on my own. I need a Teacher. I need a Counselor. I need a Helper. I believe your spirit can help me, just as Jesus promised. Let the Holy Spirit touch my mind and ignite my heart through Jesus Christ, Amen.

My letter to God in my waiting for my husband years before I met Moe (yes, God does answer prayers).

Pray for your spouse from head to toe and, yes, even before you meet your spouse. If you are married, pray daily for your spouse from head to toe.

My dearest love, Jesus,

You have shown me what true love in my heart is by loving you, Jesus, and I thank you endlessly.

Thank you for catching each tear, for understanding my desires of my heart, and for helping me to see they are not selfish. Lord, I long for and yearn for a husband brought to me from you. Someone who loves you as much as I do. Someone, Lord, I can share your love with together. Lord, I long to love him through you with unconditional love.

Lord, I pray this man from you is brought into my life, in your precious name. I pray, Lord he knows now, wherever he may be, that I already love him even though I don't know him yet. Lord, I pray for his greater good. Lord, I pray for healing upon his heart.

Lord, please help me in this time of waiting and loneliness. Lord, please give us a peace that passes all understanding.

Lord, I love you so much. You are my life and my everything.

Love, Your girl

Lord, please clothe me in compassion, kindness, humility, stillness, confidence, patience, and love. Please, Lord, clothe me in the fruit of the spirit.

Lord, please remove hurts, haughtiness, and grudges from having any definition of me.

Dear Lord,

I now put on, with thanks, the armor which you have provided for me.

Girding myself with the belt of truth, binding up all that is vulnerable of my femininity.

First, my need to be pursued and fought for. Thank you, Lord, for daily pursuing me and fighting for me as well.

Grant me eyes to see each day, to live in the bigness of your story.

I ask you to continue to reveal and confirm what you desire to do through me.

May this day be an offering of love poured out before you on the altar of my life.

Lord, help me to not stop moving forward on our path together. I tend to run and hide if my heart gets broken.

Help me to strive onward to grow closer to you, God.

When you lead me to areas that take me out of the boat that I am comfortable in, help me to let go of gripping the side of the boat, stand up, and step out of the boat, walking onward, even among the waves I will face, knowing that you love me, and I will be just fine.

Love, Your girl

Dear God,

Please remind me that one page of a book does not define the entire book. We get to enjoy each page. Each page makes up the book. One page does not define us. We are a process, a glorious journey full of God moments; one by one, strengthening our trust in you on this journey to heaven that starts right here on earth. Thank you for the journey, Lord. Sometimes, in the endings, we find beginnings.

Love, Your girl

Journal Entries, Scriptures, and Inspirations

"I'm a little pencil in the hand of a writing God,
who is sending a love letter to the world."[30]
—MOTHER TERESA OF CALCUTTA

Genesis 18:27, "Then Abraham spoke again. 'Since I have begun, let me speak further to my Lord, even though I am but dust and ashes.[31] (NLT)

1 Timothy 2:8, "Therefore I want the men everywhere to pray, lifting up holy hands without anger or disputing."[32] (NIV)

"Heart is a call to cultivate the beauty you hold inside and to
unveil this beautiful heart on behalf of others[33]."
—FROM THE RANSOMED HEART/JOHN ELDREDGE

---

30   See footnotes.
31   NLT, See footnotes.
32   NIV, See footnotes.
33   See footnotes.

"Pen and Paper"

Pen and paper, so good to keep near,
I look back on something I journaled that I feared.
The paper revealed my feelings at that time,
It reminded me of pretending to be a meme.

But, You God, are always there,
Forever for me you care.
Jesus, I finally took a hold of your hand,
You are the leader of my band!

Help me never to stop writing love letters to you, God.
To be in your will, I could see you give a nod.
For in the writings I can see,
Although I am not yet where I want to be;
I am not where I used to be!

Notes/How This Applies:

Take the Next Step Idea: Write your letter to God:

God created you! How amazing you are! Whether soaring or still, you are sealed in God's constant love!

Write a handwritten letter to someone you love, or someone you are praying for. Pray about sending it. Follow God's guidance to hand deliver your letter, mail it, or keep it in a special place for you to remember them.

Often, trusting comes with ease when all our plans go along as we intend; however, sometimes, life takes side roads we would have never seen coming.

Chapter 5

Seashells, Love, and Hearts In the Sand

Let's journey back to the day I met my love, the one I had prayed for. We were introduced by mutual friends who both kept telling us we just had to meet each other. I am thankful for smart, good friends!

Moe and I talked on the phone every day since the first phone call that started our journey. On one of our phone conversations, after talking on the phone for several weeks, he asked me about spending a day together on a Saturday.

I could hardly wait! Finally, the beautiful Saturday arrived! I looked out my window and saw this handsome country boy wearing a ballcap walking up to my door! There was my heart's first flip! Little did I know how many more "heart flips" were to happen and that one day, he would be my husband!

He drove from Virginia, and we spent the day seeing some favorite sights of my hometown, including yes, a hardware

store and a candy store! We ate at one of our best-known bar-
becue restaurants, and then went to a racing museum. At the
end of the day, we laughed and said that was our first all-day
date, and we both looked forward to many more!

Before long, I was climbing hunting stands, loving each
and every moment with Moe! I went turkey hunting, deer
hunting, fishing (with my pink tackle box), and rabbit hunting. I was dressed in my pink camo hunting bibs Moe had
bought me. I had mastered adjusting my hair through my
pink camo hat also. He was amazed how much I loved being
with him! I was so thankful for the love God sent me, straight
from Virginia!

God gave me a love story! A love story of realness; a man
I always dreamed of! So full of love, Moe amazed me how he
showed his concern for others and his love for God and his
family.

His strength, along with humbleness amazed me! He always worked hard and knew how to enjoy life to the fullest!
This book would have one million chapters if I would write all
the amazing qualities he held within.

And his eyes, oh, his eyes; they saw straight through to my
heart and soul. When we hugged, I felt two hearts merge into
one.

He introduced me to hunting, fishing, and yes, loving every day! He taught me how to truly enjoy life to the fullest and
enjoy God's beautiful outdoors!

I never dreamed I would climb into a tree wearing camos
and sit right by him looking for sixteen pointers at four in the
morning! OK, I might be stretching the size of the buck by a
few points, but I was there right beside him! I even learned to
track a deer! As long as Moe was beside me, I felt safe. I knew,

oh how I knew, he was the one! I patiently waited for him to be led by God for the next step, knowing God would lead him to change his title of boyfriend to fiance!

Then, after we had been dating for several years, the day came! Early one morning, we headed out to the woods to hunt. Not only the moonlight guided my steps, Moe guided me! I held on to his strong arm in his thick camo jacket as he guided me through the dark woods. I asked, "Honey, how do you know where to go in the dark?" He responded, "Honey, I have walked these woods so much, I just know." My love, so deep for him, along with my trust, would have followed his footsteps anywhere!

We reached our destination! I took out my small flashlight in my pocket and shined it up to the sky, and there it was! A very high tree stand with small metal steps I was to climb! Shaking at the thought of heights, I took one step at a time, knowing the steep climb would be worth the destination. Let me also mention that this was a year to the day that I had my neck injury. I guess I believed a good way to celebrate my neck injury recovery was to climb a tree! Knowing Moe was right behind me helped me to be brave.

I climbed as slowly as a turtle, but finally, reached my seat, a nice metal seat that would serve as my lookout station for the next six hours or until "we" got a deer! I took a seat and held a very tight grip to the side of the tree stand that was attached to a strong steady tree. If trees had eyes, I am pretty sure the tree was laughing at me! We sat for hours. As I quietly sat in the tree stand reading my book and listening for the sound of that sixteen point buck (that were actually squirrels most of the time), I always had a feeling of peace, knowing I was right where I belonged. I looked up from my book and saw leaves in the shape of hearts ahead of me. It reminded me of Moe and me going to the beach years ago after we had dated for several months. We were collecting seashells along the shore, and we saw hearts along the shoreline, hundreds of them as if God had drawn them in the sand for us. I felt like the most blessed girlfriend in the world. I felt a love I cannot express into words. I smiled so big, and all who knew me saw love in my eyes.

After hanging out in the tree for hours, there it was!! This beautiful buck! Moe, with such precision, had gotten a seven pointer! We climbed out of the stand with such excitement! We walked over to where the deer was, and as Moe attended to the deer, I turned to look for more deer. I turned back around, and then, to my surprise, Moe was on one knee! He took a beautiful shiny diamond ring out of his camo hunting jacket and asked me to marry him!

He asked and I said YES!!!! Well, needless to say, I didn't even see deer after that! All I saw was my dear, and I could not take my eyes off my ring glowing! Moe had purchased the ring months ago, and he had been waiting for just the right time.

In the woods of Virginia, on a beautiful November day, surrounded by beautiful leaves, days before Thanksgiving, I was a bride-to-be of the perfect man God had chosen for me! Oh, and remember the letters to God I had written? Moe was an answer to all I had written in my letters to God! Now, God was writing my love letter back to me!

His calm loving spirit, intertwined with his amazing strength, amazed me!

When I met Moe, I fell so in love!! This was the first time I was in love! Each time I saw Moe, I would jump into his arms!

We married on September 12, 2015 after dating almost four years. Our wedding was my dream wedding outside by the lake at Fairy Stone State Park in Virginia. The planning that went into the wedding was so much fun. We wrote and gave each other love letters the day of our wedding. My smile was as large as the vast ocean! There was total peace and contentment inside my spirit. God had answered my prayers!

We honeymooned in Gatlinburg, Tennessee, for a week in a beautiful cabin, and even stayed an extra day! We took horseback rides through the beautiful Tennessee mountains, and had such an amazing week!

In July 2016, not even a year since our wedding date, my husband began to have some symptoms that took us to his physician. The doctor ordered a biopsy and advised us to return a week later to receive the results. When we returned to the office, the doctors gave us the results and said that word cancer. My knees went weak. I couldn't even say the word for the longest time. I tried to be strong and hold back my tears, and finally, I just cried and cried. My husband took my hand and looked into my eyes and said, "Honey, you always say trust God. Well, we get to trust God with this."

The diagnosis of cancer changed our world, but not our love. I would have moved a mountain for my husband. As my husband would put his hunting boots on, I thought those boots were combat boots to beat the cancer!

Our days now involved trips to cancer centers, hospitalizations, hope one minute the chemo was working, and tears the next minute when his body was growing so tired of the treatments. Not a moment did my husband voice a complaint. He always cared about others and spoke to complete strangers with love and respect. Even during his worst days, he always had concern and care for others.

During one of our hospitalizations during the middle of the night, the doctors sent Moe for a scan. I walked along, holding his hand. When they took Moe into the procedure room, I slid down the wall and grabbed my knees and cried out to God to please not take my husband away from me. His blood pressure had dropped that night so low, I was so scared!

After his scan, we returned to the hospital room. There was a nurse standing in the hallway, and she saw the tears in my eyes. She gave me a hug and told me she was there for me. Once my husband got settled back in the room, I literally sat by my husband's bedside, placing my hands on his legs, begging God to take all my strength inside me and give it all to my husband, as his weakness had increased.

Immediately after the prayer, my husband started feeling so much better, we were discharged home, and my husband was able to see his family and friends in the following weeks. I still believed that God would take my husband's cancer and throw it in the depths of the sea to be gone forever as I had asked on that day we were sitting on the shore fishing.

The doctor advised hospice care. I still believed the cancer would go away and we would beat the cancer. Cancer is like a fire, blazing at heights at times, trying to demand attention to its fiery flames. My husband and I showed cancer that love prevails. Cancer cannot steal love!

One day, my husband told me he wanted to be baptized that day. I called the Pastor that was so faithful to visit Moe during his illness . He told us to drive on to the church and that he was honored to baptize my husband. It was beautiful watching Moe be baptized!

I still believed God would toss this cancer into the depths of the sea and our lives would be like before. I still believed!

This chapter's journal section is a series of writings written on the oncology floor, hospice days, or wherever, whenever God poured words into my pen onto my paper.

Many times, as I sat in a hospital or cancer center's waiting rooms, I would feel God's presence and begin to journal when led. I am but a penholder. God is the writer. God, "Are you still writing my love letter?" I would wonder. I knew in my heart, God was still writing my love letter.

Going through valleys with ones you love brings you even closer. Our love continued to be strengthened every hour.

We were transferred from home to the hospice house in the very early morning hours of April 26, 2017 by the advice of our hospice doctor. My husband was able to stay at home during hospice care until the day when the hospice doctor admitted us to the hospice house. My husband, with me by his side, was given a room right next to the family waiting room, and we had such amazing nurses all along our journey who were angels.

We were given warm blankets that were knitted together with love. As I sat beside my husband, he whispered the words, "I love you." I held his hand and sang to him. I thanked him for the love he had shown me and for being the best husband, and I told him how much I loved him! Those were the last words my husband spoke, as his body rested. I thanked my husband for being my everything, my strength, and my love! I whispered, "I love you so much, Honey and I always will."

I still believed a doctor would come into the hospice room and give us a plan for all to get better. Hours later, instead, a nurse came into our room and said she could tell by my husband's breathing that he was closer to going into the arms of Jesus. Family, friends, and pastors spent the day with us, which was beautiful.

Even through it all, I still believed the doctor would show up with a plan of care. I was still hoping God would heal the cancer. I was still believing in a miracle.

On the afternoon of April 26, 2017 at 4:10 in the afternoon, with me and family by his side, my amazing, handsome husband's eyes revealed a look of amazement!

My amazing husband won his battle with cancer and peacefully went to be with Jesus.

I felt my husband's spirit leap inside my spirit, and I could feel as though he was leaping out of cancer into Jesus' healing arms. As complete healing took place for my husband and his desire to feel young again was granted, my knees felt weak and I sank to the floor. A journey of healing for one, a journey of grief for another.

In the days ahead, I thought why wasn't my love, faith, and belief enough to heal Moe's cancer? My love for him could have moved mountains. Why did it not heal his cancer?

Then, I realized I am not God.

God did heal my husband, just not in the way I desired. I wanted to keep my husband with me, healed and feeling young again.

At that time, I did not have the energy to stoop down and pick up the pieces of my broken heart. God reached down, stooped down alongside me, and swept up the broken pieces. God picked up all the frayed and jagged edges and gently held them, all while embracing me within the broken pieces. God held me and caught each tear, and once again whispered, "I am here, my sweet precious child. Two by two together, I hold you and love you. You are never alone. Two by two, I go along with you."

Yes, even broken seashells are beautiful.

The following pages are a series of journal writings during our journey of hope, also known as cancer.

Journal Entries, Scriptures, and Inspirations

The Waiting Rooms

Waiting room;
Sky above;
Some people are talking, as to try to cheer up a loved one.
Some quiet, all on their journey.

Above, beautiful blue sky, clouds moving,
Moving forward, I notice they don't stop or move backward.
I am wishing the clouds would stop. How I wish time would
stop on the best days.
Hello, heart-shaped cloud; I see you.

God's amazing love surrounds,
Side by side, heartbeat in hand.
Walks in hall, ribbons for cancer survivors,
Each breath survived.
I tie a ribbon for love on the oncology floor ribbon tree for
the love of my life, my husband, and I pray and hope; I hope
and pray.

With hearts and heartbeat in hand.

"Blessed Girl in a Cancer Ward"

Childlike faith surrounds heart shape;
How can I be in a cancer ward and feel like
The most blessed girl in the world?

God's beauty is here.
How can I feel so protected and loved?
God's beauty is here.

Feel like a protected child of God,
Whose parents are standing up for her.
Amazing Power of Prayer.

God's beauty is here.
(Written 02/20/2017 as I sat by my husband's side on the oncology floor.)

And The Birds Danced ...

Sun appeared
Birds danced
Broken shells
Beautiful still
Brokenness
Beautiful still
Smell of sea
Remember
Heartbeat in hand
Remember

Fishing
Remember
Swimming dolphins
Remember
Jesus bowed
and
Birds danced
Thankfulness
Hearts
Love
Remember
02/13/2017 Remembering this journal entry as I sat on an oncology ward that was written months before at the beach.

Psalm 27:13-14 "I remain confident of this: I will see the goodness of the Lord in the land of the living. Wait for the Lord; be strong and take heart and wait for the Lord."[34] (NIV)

Psalm 5:3 "In the morning, Lord, you hear my voice; in the morning I lay my requests before you and wait expectantly."[35] (NIV)

Psalm 5:3 "My voice shalt thou hear in the morning, O Lord; in the morning will I direct my prayer unto thee, and will look up."[36](KJV)

---

34 NIV, See footnotes.
35 NIV, See footnotes.
36 KJV, See footnotes.

Psalm 3:3 "But you, O Lord, are a shield around me; you are my glory, the one who holds my head high."[37] (NLT)

---

37 NLT, See footnotes.

Notes/How This Applies:

Take The Next Step Ideas: Think or write about a time when your life took you to an unexpected place you did not think you were ready for:
Have you envisioned a plan for unexpected events?

Who do you or who would you reach out to in moments of struggle?

Imagine God picking up shattered, broken pieces with frayed edges and God holding them and embracing you cupped in His love and care.

Pray about each part of your life that has caused you hurt. Some examples may be disappointments, unfulfilled dreams, a person, an event, etc.

You may need to peel down layers to get to them.

Feel free to take some time and make notes.

Consider writing each one in your notes or journal.

If you are not comfortable writing them, consider speaking them. Or, if you would rather, just sit still in a quiet place and be in God's presence.

Pray about any person or any circumstance that has caused you hurt.

Chapter 6

Flights, Landings, and Torn Sails

So, it's my first day leaving the house. Should I call this a practice day of how to get used to "this being by myself stuff?" My big smile is gone. I am in a club called the widows club that I did not want or ask for membership in. How will I carry on?

My teenage daughter and her friends want to go shopping at a mall. Here I am, a single mom again. I had this role for many years after my divorce from my first husband; but then, it was my choice. It was an escape from my tumultuous first marriage. However, now I do not want to be single! I had found the love of my life and was finally happy and content through the love of Jesus. Now, I am a widow!!

For my daughter, I venture out of the house. I developed a plan for the day that was ahead. I will not go near the Bass Pro Shops where my beloved husband, Moe, and I loved to go.

Moe and I used to love going to the Bass Pro Shops and dream of buying a new boat one day.

I picked up my daughter's friends and drove us all to the mall. When we reached the mall, not seeing the inside tears I hid, my daughter and her friends hurriedly ran to their favorite shops full of excitement for this day out!

I found a table in the food court and sat down. I watched others in the food court around me who seemed to be going about their lives. I watched families, with excitement, place their children on the merry-go-round and laugh. I feel I am outside looking in. There must be a glass in between me and them. Maybe I am watching a movie reel go round and round. How can they laugh? Why do I cry all the time?

My life seemed over. I straighten myself up in my seat at my table surrounded by empty seats. One person even came up to my table and asked me, "Are you going to need these chairs?" I respond, holding back my tears, "No, help yourself to the chairs, sir." The man picked up the empty chairs at my table and took them to his family to add more chairs.

I did not even feel I had a family anymore! I felt broken! I felt that I was being kicked while I was down. All this stranger did was ask for a chair, and it felt like a knife in my side! The smallest triggers could cause tears to roll down my cheek.

At the table next to me, a wife is complaining about her husband to her friend. I overheard her say that her husband forgot her grocery list because he had his mind on golfing. Really!! I wanted to scream at this lady I didn't even know, wanting to say, "Treasure your husband, lady!! Treasure him!! Do you know how much I wish my husband was here?" However, I remained quiet. At times, to be honest, when I would hear women complaining about their husbands, I wish

I could stop them and say, "Please stop! Please stop complaining! Don't you know how blessed you are?"

This day, God was already at my table for one, waiting for my heart. He gave me the strength to walk to the table. He will give me the strength to face this hour and all the hours to come. I look around the mall at all the people who are paired together. I felt despair, but say, "No!" in my spirit. "No, Debra. This time, you are not going to cry again." I tell myself, "Just hold the tears in until you get to the car."

Then, I decided, as I waited on my daughter and her friends, I should go to a new location, perhaps to the cinema, which is located inside the mall, to watch a movie. I leave the food court and walk to the indoor cinema. I approach the ticket counter and say, "Ticket for one," holding back my tears. My heart sobs inside as I walk to theater number three. "I am trying to do this, Honey," I whisper to my husband in heaven. Somehow, I know Moe would have done much better at this grief thing than me. He would have been so much stronger.

Yesterday, I sat holding my husband's camo bibs he used to wear while hunting, and I sobbed into them, saying, "I will never wash them," praying they continue to have his scent. Today, I am trying to hold it together the best I can. He should be here with me! He was young! He was strong! He was healthy! He lived healthy! This should not have happened! We were newlyweds!

My hospice counselor had been encouraging me to verbalize and describe my grief journey. One day, a friend of mine asked how I was doing. I responded with, "Grief stinks!! This grief thing stinks like rotten lemons that have been left outside for years on the hottest days of the year!!"

I struggled with verbalizing my grief and kept it deep inside me for the longest time. Grief would reveal itself at times I was not prepared. I am not sure how you would prepare anyway.

Once, I was in a store and it started raining. I began to cry! My husband Moe would always call to tell me to be careful when the weather was bad. When I was driving, he would ask me to call and let him know I made it home OK. Standing there in the store, I cried and cried because I felt no one cared or would even know if I got home! I felt I was alone to weather the storm! My sails sure felt torn; however, God, my anchor was holding me!

Each time I went to the grocery store, I cried. I would see people who knew me start down an aisle and turn and go the other way when they saw me. I knew they just didn't know what to say to me. I do not know why the grocery store was a trigger for tears, but it was for me.

Many days, I could not feel my arms or legs. I felt numb. My heart literally hurt. I hurt deep in my chest!

How I walked to the cinema that day at the mall, I am not sure! My legs felt heavy, as though I had exercised for hours! Grief is tiring! I was tired! I thought maybe going to watch a movie would help. Maybe entering an imaginary place for just a while would be a good thing to try. Maybe, I could set grief aside for a while.

The minute I sat down in the theater, I missed Moe sitting beside me, as we loved going to the movies! Moe liked real life movies. I liked romantic comedies. Honestly, I do not remember the movie that I saw to this day. But, I sat in front of a screen with noises for a while. I noticed the lady sitting behind me in the cinema is also by herself. We both put our heads together and figured out how the recliners worked in theater number three. We both laugh for a moment. I wonder, does her heart hurt also? But, for now, she brings a smile. I honestly did not know I had a smile that existed inside of me anymore.

Journal Entries, Scriptures, and Inspirations

"The Deer Stands Alone"

The deer, oh so strong;
Standing all alone;
The path, oh I wonder, have you trod?

The eyes of two in excitement behold you;
One full of wisdom, as to know your every move.
One takes you in with wonder,
Both heartbeats speed up.

You look up in the tall stand;
We smile.
One talks to you in a whisper, as if she knows your thoughts;
She waits quietly in wonderment of the next moment,
She asks him, the one with wisdom,
Will you let him go?

You see, his path, oh to trod!
With His creator more to see.
Because He loves, he lets go
For more journeys call his name.

For the deer now stands alone.

After the death of my second husband, I revisited feelings of aloneness that tried to take me back to "my own little world." Thankfully, this time, I felt my Savior alongside me, and I did not stay in the place of feeling like a victim for the length I used to. I see Jesus as my life preserver, and as I grow in my relationship with Jesus, He is more reachable. I learned to grab the lifeline to the life preserver much quicker. But, oh how I wish that I would never have let go of my lifeline in the first place. I am thankful for God's never-ending grace, and God doesn't give up on us!

"I went to the woods because I wished to live deliberately, to front only the essential facts of life, and see if I could not learn what it had to teach, and not, when I came to die, discover that I had not lived."[38]
—HENRY DAVID THOREAU

God cares for us. God carries us.

"When you pass through the waters, I will be with you; and when you pass through the rivers, they will not sweep over you. When you walk through the fire, you will not be burned; the flames will not set you ablaze."[39]
—ISAIAH 43:2 (NIV)

"The Sovereign Lord is my strength; he makes my feet like the feet of a deer, he enables me to tread on the heights."[40]
—HABAKKUK 3:19 (NIV)

---

38 See footnotes.
39 NIV, See footnotes.
40 NIV, See footnotes.

I love you, Honey.

I bet you are fishing today with Jesus.

I think of heaven a lot now.

You are in my heart alive.

And me, I just need to breathe, my goal for this minute.

Author's note: *I wrote this one month after my husband went to his heavenly home.*

"We discovered that you can carry on a conversation and cry at the same time. You can cry while vacuuming the living room. You can cry when ordering pizza over the phone, although the conversation is longer and more confusing than it otherwise would be and you sometimes get a topping you didn't order.

You can weep while coloring. Your scribble might have splotches where my tears fall when I color with my child.

Then, you have that moment you think you are OK and you are reminded how much you miss him and you aren't just leaking water from your eyes.

You are frozen and grief is a splintery thing the size of a telephone pole shoving its way through your chest."[41]

From the book, *Here If You Need Me by Kate Braestrup* in grief for her husband.

---

41 See footnotes.

"Silence Screams"

Silence is so LOUD!
Silence screams at times,
How terrible the pain is!
No one; there is no one!
Not even one who cares, except God!
God always cares and carries.

Who wants to talk to a washed-up widow?
No one, not one!
God hears.
God walks alongside.
Even in the silence, there are screams!

"Birthday Cakes and Soggy Candles"

I cried all day today. I drove to your resting place, Honey, to put a birthday flag out. I cried to my husband, telling him he is the strong one and he should be the one left here behind.

His spirit reassured me.

The sun breaks through the trees, as if to shine rays right on me. I feel warmth. I feel his spirit. I feel his whisper of how young he feels and how happy he is there in heaven. He is well nourished by the most amazing nourishment there is. His heart is full. I see a heart-shaped leaf as I look at the tree by his resting place. He is my heart.

His spirit reassures me.

How I miss his touch, his smiles, his eyes, his dimples, his strong arms, and his hugs so tightly wrapped around with me in the middle, feeling safe and secure. I am tired!

His spirit guides me.

It's my husband's birthday today, another day my heart aches missing him. "Happy Birthday," the girls and I say, as we look up to heaven, placing balloons and a birthday flag and flowers on his resting place.

My daughter finds a dollar bill on the ground, and she looks up to heaven and says, "Hey, thanks Dad!"

His spirit makes us smile just in time.

The sunshine rays pour over us as to speak to me.
We speak of heaven, the girls and I, and
We wonder: Is there food in heaven? Are there four wheelers in heaven? What are you doing right now, Honey in heaven?
You have everything in eternal life.
You are young again.

My heart smiles as I think of love alongside the rays of sunshine.
We return home to prepare a birthday meal that, "Dad would like," my daughter says.
So, steak it is. We miss his grilling expertise, but we try.

"We love you, Honey! Happy happy birthday, my love, my ray of sunshine."

05/20/2017 (my husband's fifty-third birthday)

"When you survive loss, everyone is quick to tell you how strong you are, and how tough you must be. But, actually, no one has a choice to survive grief do they? It's not optional. You just have to cry in the shower, sob in your pillow and pray you will make it."[42]

—ZOE CLARK-COATES

"Different Oars Through The Waves"

In the same boat,
We all have different oars.
How is your oar paddling through,
I wonder from across the boat?

Grief waves are there;
Some small,
Some medium,
Some tsunami waves!

This one task, let me complete.
I try to focus, although the grief veil darkens.

As each oar moves in direction,
It has touched that ripple in the waves.
On to another wave; the long journey holds more,
Each wave touched by the oar.

06/12/2017

---

42 See footnotes.

Author's note: *My hospice grief counselor encouraged me to talk to others who were also going through grief. He said, "It is like you all are on a boat, each with your own oar. I would like for you to ask others in the boat how their oars are moving along." This encouraged me to join GriefShare at my church.*

Belt of truth;
Helmet of salvation;
Clothed with truth, righteousness, prayer, and faith.
Shoes of peace;
Carry the sword of spirit;
The Word of God provides a pathway.

Keep God's word before us.

I am trying to lean into God's word, my guidemap.
I can almost hear my pastor say, "The word of God, for the people of God; thanks be to God."

I am learning to take a step forward standing on the word of God, leaning into faith, and progressing on this new path.

"Christian hope isn't about looking around at the state of things now and trying to imagine where it's all going. It's not about trying to calculate the future from the present. It's about breathing now the fresh air, toasting the spices and sipping the wine of the feast to come."[43]
—A Place for Truth: Leading Thinkers Explore Life's Hardest Questions (Dallas Willard, editor)

Giant Waves Hurt

Big giant waves pounding upon me,
Throwing me under the water
Forcing me down, I can't breathe!
My dreams are shattered!
Where is his voice? I long for his presence,
his arms, and his eyes
The waves are drowning me!
I cannot see the shore anymore, it seems like forever!
I can no longer see the shore.

Author's note: *This was written two weeks after my husband was called to his forever home. I felt I was drowning, the pain so deep missing him.*

Even in the midst of my feeling of drowning, I was sensing God reassuring my spirit that I would be able to get out of this storm and soar to the top of the mountains where my wings would take flight.

---

43 See footnotes.

Psalm 94:18-19 (NIV) "When I said, 'My foot is slipping,' your unfailing love, Lord, supported me."

"When anxiety was great within me, your consolation brought me joy." [44]

"Thrift Stores Even Make Me Cry"

Well, my one dollar thrift store find
Even makes me cry!

Every second my heart beats, it misses,
Misses the one who made me smile.
Misses the one who held me, reassured me, and loved me;
Misses the one who protected me from the madness;
Misses my best friend, my love, and my protector.

My husband lives in my heart now.
Cancer, you didn't take that!

Each heartbeat combines with my husband's;
So yes, there is hope and a future.
Right now, each holiday brings more tears;
Along with each sunrise.

However,

Because our one and only Son rose;

---

44 NIV, See footnotes.

I will dance with my husband one day!
And one day, our hands will be clenched together.

Again.

Heartbeat in hand, us both with the Father, Son, and Holy Spirit.

He is saving a place for me.

Heartbeat in hand.

During my GriefShare class, we were encouraged to write a letter to our friends and family with the goal of sharing a glimpse into our world of grief. Here is my letter:

Dear friend, family, or even a person who doesn't know me who may see me crying,

I recently suffered a devastating loss. I am on a grief journey that can be and is often very unpredictable. This journey may last years, and I will cry from time to time. I do not apologize for my tears, since they are not a sign of weakness or a lack of faith. They are God's gift to me to express the extent of my love and my loss. These tears are also a sign I am on a journey of deep love.

At times, you may see me smiling as I join in conversation about my handsome hero husband, as I so enjoy speaking of his life and all he taught me about living.

At other times, you may see I seem angry for no apparent reason. Sometimes, I am not sure why. Other times, I may be thinking how can the world continue when mine seemed to end?

It can be exhausting trying to figure this all out, and grief is exhausting enough. So best to not try to figure it (or me) out.

My emotions can be intense at times because of my grief. If I do not always make sense to you, please forgive me and be patient with me. If I repeat myself, forget things, or seem to be miles away, please be patient with me.

The death of my husband, my love, feels as though, at times, it has ended my life. However, my husband loved life, and for him and others, I will lean on God to accept each heartbeat God gives me.

My husband's strength was amazing! When he held me, my heart melted into his. We loved to hold hands, and I still remember feeling his heartbeat in my hands. While at the cancer center, the staff would say we were the cutest couple, as they could tell we were newlyweds. We held hands clenched tightly in the hallway, while my husband would ask others how they were as they each passed us in the hallway. He treated complete strangers with respect and love, and was always thinking of others. He never complained through his cancer journey or anytime in his life. He portrayed the peace of Jesus. He set an example for me to live life fully, to treat others as you like to be treated, and to rely on God. He also taught me how to go into the loving arms of Jesus with dignity, grace, and the peace of God when God calls me home to heaven.

Our love, like the strength of an oak tree (with heart leaves of course), will continue to thrive and spread.

So, when sadness across your spirit and eyes may come as you see grief in my eyes, I ask you to celebrate this love that has been given to me. The greatest of these is love. My life is blessed.

I have loved and love the wonderful name of Jesus. My husband showed me to love the wonderful name "husband." I am blessed. My husband was an amazing, loving husband, and I feel I was an amazing, loving wife to him. I was by his side and he by mine.

Always be yourself and treasure how God made you, for He knows the number of hairs on your head and he knitted you together to be treasured and to treasure each breath. Love a lot and treasure your loved ones each chance you get. Laugh a lot too.

Why am I writing this? I am not sure, other than God pressed into my heart to send this to you. That is how much I treasure you.

"And so, the birds danced. In God's light and presence, the birds ... danced."

God's abundant blessings upon you always.

Love, Debra

Notes/How This Applies:

Take The Next Step Idea:

Think about a time you dropped something that scattered into a million pieces. You probably were working on a goal, and cleaning up shattered pieces was not in your plan for the day. It took time to stop and clean up these pieces. The pieces demanded attention. Sure, you could have chosen to leave the pieces on the floor and step over them, or go around them, or maybe totally avoid them by not ever going into the place where the pieces remain.

Imagine pieces of shattered dreams in your life. Have you swept them up, paying no attention to them, and regarded them as "oh well, that's life?" Or are they still on the floor, shattered and not looked upon anymore?

What if we always left these shattered pieces and more and more pieces were added?

Name, if you would like, times you have experienced shattered dreams. Where are the pieces?

Even in my days of hope, I grieve.

Chapter 7

Dancing Over the Sea With Broken Wings

Kindness often starts with us being kind to ourselves and then to others. Over the grief journey, it has helped me to not have unreachable goals. I learned to set realistic goals. Honestly, some days, walking to the mailbox was a marathon! Other days, I was able to focus, as I felt the grief veil was not as heavy, and I accomplished items on my list. I learned to take one day at a time, one step at a time.

I learned to have a way out. For example, if I felt up to lunch with a friend, I would drive myself, in case the tear train flowed from my eyes and I needed to retreat to my comfort zone! I also learned that it was OK to not be OK some days. There is no report card for grief. Nobody is graded along their grief journey.

I found that in the first year after my husband Moe went to his heavenly home, I placed myself in "Grief Honor College"!

I read every book on grief I could find. My hospice counselor told me, "You are working very hard at this grief thing!" He reminded me it would be nice to just read a book I would enjoy. I believe I was trying to excel at this process, as if I thought I would graduate one day. I started taking a deep breath and accepting myself right where I was.

For a season, attending GriefShare and hospice counseling helped, and I did learn many tools to have in my tool box to deal with the unpredictable ways of grief. I did learn it is OK to express to the best of my ability how I was feeling. I had no problem telling God the way I felt! I figured He knew anyway. Although I always loved God, I would tell him, crying out at times, that I wanted my husband back here with me!! I miss my husband so much!

I have found the grief process is not as "all consuming" as it was years ago. I think of the love my husband Moe and I share, and thank God for such a love every day.

It's almost Valentine's Day again, and I count the number four. Four years missing my husband, especially on this day and other days that hold special memories. It's been five years since Moe said he wanted to take me to the beach for Valentine's weekend. God woke me up each morning that Valentine weekend in 2017 to see the sunrise. There were some days after Moe died I didn't want to see another sunrise.

I would think back to our last trip to the beach and my walk along the shore. The sight of the beautiful birds taking flight when the glowing sun arose gave me hope. I remembered how the birds soared at the gift of the new day. I remembered how graceful the birds flew. Such a graceful dance for God's delight.

It was there on that shore Valentine's weekend 2017 that God gave me the title for this book. The many journal entries came from God over the next four years. God gave me the title, and He filled the pages, all along giving me hope.

Today, on my fourth Valentine's weekend after Moe's death, I write "The Tears and The Smile" to just give a glimpse of hope to those grieving. Some days will feel like tsunami waves of grief, and then one day, when you least expect it, God turns your thinking to thankfulness instead of feeling like someone was taken from you. Your heart, although always thankful for this gift of love, starts to focus more on the thankfulness for a great love given to you and the gift of many precious memories. Oh yes, how the love continues to grow. That love will always be with you, and you will continue to miss your loved one.

On some days, I can feel his whisper of, "I love you, Honey" to my heart. On some days, I can imagine Moe saying, "I hear ya, Honey" as he would smile at me just being me. I am beginning to make the turn of expressing more thankfulness for such a love gained from him instead of me expressing my loss. My husband is not lost. I know he is with Jesus in heaven, so he is not lost. However, the loss is me missing his presence. I lost the next time for him to hold my hand, feeling his heartbeat in my hand. All these moments will remain in my heart and spirit forever.

He is a gain of love that lasts forever within me. Instead of feeling he was taken away from me, I started to see what a beautiful gift was given to me to be so in love with him! I, even among the veil of grief, realized the beautiful gift God chose for us to be husband and wife.

I am so thankful God chose us for each other, a gift always to be cherished until our hearts again collide together in heaven in the presence of the gift giver, our abundant loving Father, Son, and Holy Spirit. Until then, my heart will dream of the day I will dance like the birds soaring over the ocean with healed wings transformed by my living hope, Jesus Christ.

"And the greatest of these is love."

Journal Entries, Scriptures, and Inspirations

"The Tears and The Smile"

They collide;
The tears and the smile.

The tears of deeply missing
Looking into his eyes,
Hearing his voice,
Two hearts melting into one.

They collide;
The tears and the smile.

The smile across my face;
I thought I would never smile again.
But there it is! Among the veil,
I almost let it escape unnoticed.

That memory yielded a smile,
To be cherished even if tears still flow.

Thankfulness for a love always,
Cherish I will.
The tears and the smile collide at
the intersection of grief and healing.

The Maker of our hearts hears and heals.
If only a Band-Aid at a time, He heals and He hears.
He carries, He cares.

Thankful for our Healer.
Thankful for love.
Thankful for the tears and the smile.

"Our Hearts Again Collide"

I see a picture of us and say,
"I want to go back"
To that day and stay.

I so wish cancer had not taken you away!

Away,
From holding me in your arms;
Away,
From dreams oh so strong;
Away,
From blue sparkling eyes for you;
Away,
From a woven tapestry of two into one.

In my heart, you will always be;
Here,
In my dreams and memories;
Here,

Remembrance of talks, laughs, and kisses;
Here,
Holding tight;
Here,
Awaiting again the day our hearts again collide!

And The Birds Danced

Today, I sat by my husband's resting place in my pink John Deere chair. I wonder if you have met my grandparents yet and are you fishing with my grandpa?

The wind calm and cool moves, as if I was inside the tree limbs swaying back and forth.
At times, leaves would flow from the tree almost as if the leaves were speaking to me.

My thoughts take me to the book of Ecclesiastes in the Bible.
Time and seasons.
A red bird lands on a limb;
Well nourished, as if to say my grandma has just cooked some good ole country cooking, and my husband is well nourished and able to eat.

I hear a noise in the distance;
As if a deer, sounds like an eight pointer, Honey,
Once again, it's a squirrel!

I placed fresh, beautiful, and alive flowers on top of the sun-
flowers I placed a week ago.
I love you, Honey!

The tree leaves show hearts;
The sky above shows hearts that expand, as if to say,
Live, Honey, live!

"Oh, when will my heart stop hurting?"
"When, oh, when will joy come again, Lord?"

"Let Go ... Hold On"

On to more paths to trod, he gives a nod;
Two that love not given enough time;
One a break in the path he takes; she cannot understand.

The path one to take, the other to wait
One takes the hand of his Savior as
his eyes see amazement and wonder;
The other on the path her Savior her heart He holds.

But, oh, the path, the path awaits
the two as the path still stands
Heartbeat in hand to be joined again, the wisdom and the love
For the buck, strong and steady, and the doe,
at times falling to her knees. They both await
Each await
Neither alone, for their Savior who joins them holds them
both

Take Note

Oh God, "Will I ever be able to laugh again?"
This I cannot imagine right now.

Don't sweat the small stuff;
Hug, love, and be kind.
Don't tear down;
Build up others.

Take Note

You are not promised tomorrow.
Each breath is a gift from above
Would you kick over a gift if it falls at your feet?
Imagine picking the gift up, treasuring it, and caring.

Be kind to others and yourselves.
You are treasured;
You are loved.

Faith, hope, and love; the greatest of these is love.

So, I am called a widow now.
At the same time, I am called a princess
loved by our One True King,
For whom I love and live for.

Yes, my pain is great.
Yes, each day has a wave of grief,
But God is my wave catcher who

Is riding waves alongside me.

One day, we will walk on the shore together
Where there will be one set of footprints for me.
He carries me always!
Blessings in abundance;
Appear right after thankfulness.

"Not that I have already obtained all this, or have already arrived at my goal, but I press on to take hold of that for which Christ Jesus took hold of me. Brothers and sisters, I do not consider myself yet to have taken hold of it. But one thing I do: Forgetting what is behind and straining toward what is ahead, I press on toward the goal to win the prize for which God has called me heavenward in Christ Jesus."[45] Philippians 3:12-16

I will never forget the love and the gift of my amazing husband, my handsome hero husband Moe. I will carry his love with me forever.

I will strive to move forward, to keep living in his honor, as he would want.

I will strive to keep moving forward with Jesus in all that comes our way.

---

45 NIV, See footnotes.

"The Bloom Awaits"

The rose so delicate, fragrant, and true;
Some open, some closed
Waiting on the bloom.
Oh, the joyous bloom!
Each layer revealed with time,
Jesus bowing in such a quiet, gentle, loving, and peaceful way.

Oh, the trust of the rose to the Master's hand;
On this, I will stand.

The rose in God's timing opens for an audience of One,
The One who has shown love for each season.
At times of dew, at times of drought;
God delights in all.
Forever in the drought God beholds,
Each one full of hope.
For the bloom awaits.
Each belonging to Him, the audience of One,
Of beauty in His sight,
For an audience of
His delight.

"I am the vine; you are the branches. If you remain in me and I in you, you will bear much fruit; apart from me you can do nothing." John 15:5 (NIV)[46]

---

46 NIV, See footnotes.

"May the God of hope fill you with all joy and peace as you trust in him, so that you may overflow with hope by the power of the Holy Spirit." Romans 15:13 (NIV)[47]

Envisioning

Envisioning beyond circumstances,
Faith.
So many times, I talk of waves in my life,
Sometimes, I felt I was drowning.

Water that can be life-giving and so refreshing
Also, water has the ability to take us under and drown us.

I envision during those waves God protecting,
Putting space around me,
Keeping the strong waves away until,

Until I am ready to embrace the refreshing water
Meant for good for me.

I give myself a reminder to envision looking beyond the waves,
and to envision the shore.

---

47 NIV, See footnotes.

Soldiers are not unprepared
They accept their call,
gladly wearing their full armor
They move onward.

Step Out in Faith!

We are on battlefields each day.
Lord, place our feet to be pleasing to you.
Move me onward on your path in spite of the curves.
Destination known or unknown, in God's will I desire to be!

I envision my ship in the ocean; the waves ebb and flow;
Whether the waves flow with ease or with force,
I have an anchor that holds!
No matter the path I take,
The sails whether torn or intact,
My Savior, my anchor holds my map.

HOPE: Holding Onto the Promises of Eternity

In ancient times, a form of refining involved craftsmen sitting next to a hot fire with molten gold in a crucible being stirred and skimmed to remove the impurities or dross that rose to the top of a molten metal. The resulting product is a muddy substance that is almost pure gold.

"Some of the wise will stumble, so that they may be refined, purified and made spotless until the time of the end, for it will still come at the appointed time." Daniel 11:35 (NIV)[48]

Refined, becoming refined
Seeing me as God sees me.
Threads and tears, many colors once were
To God a sight of beautiful tapestry.

"Suffering doesn't destroy faith, it refines it."[49]
—MELISSA CAMP (FIRST WIFE OF JEREMY CAMP,
WRITTEN DURING HER JOURNEY OF CANCER,
BEFORE SHE TOUCHED HEAVEN)

Captivating
Captivated
I am starting to see me as captivating
Captivated by Jesus' love.

I am beginning to see again.

---

48 See footnote.
49 See footnotes.

"You are a woman. An image bearer of God,
the crown of creation. You were chosen and
you are dearly loved. You are sought after, pursued and
romanced by Jesus. As a woman who has been
ransomed and redeemed you can be strong and tender."[50]
—CAPTIVATING: UNVEILING THE MYSTERY OF A WOMAN'S
SOUL (BOOK BY JOHN AND STASI ELDREDGE)

Revelation 21:4, "He will wipe every tear from their eyes. There will be no more death or mourning or crying or pain, for the old order of things has passed away. Death will be no more; grief, crying, and pain will be no more, because the previous things have passed away."[51]

I wrote this journal entry as a reminder, be kind to me as well as others.

Kindness

A look of surprise you can see upon the face;
The loving act of kindness from a stranger has been shown.
As if a message to say God is in this place.

Kindness needs no words at times;
Maybe a smile, a nod, a green light to go, or a signal to wait.
Kindness can reveal grace and is never a day late.

---

50 See footnotes.
51 NIV, See footnotes.

Kindness can be a Band-Aid to a broken heart;
Or a lift to a fallen bird to once again depart.
As Christians, God's kindness in our hearts we cannot hide
A gentle reminder of the fruit of the spirit always to guide.

Love Out Loud

What freedom, what joy to behold
Striving to gently love out loud with Jesus and be more bold!

You see how we have the love of Christ so strong;
Oh, the joy to love with Jesus in eternity I forever long!

Laughter, tears, joys, and trials shared,
You can see how for others you truly care,
Thank you, Lord for your blessings, help me in Jesus to shine
And remember to always be kind.

Living for Jesus in hope, love, forgiveness, faith, compassion,
and spiritual fruits;
Accepting Jesus as Savior and relying on God's word, the truth.
This truly is the key,
To live with Jesus in eternity!

So blessed with a life striving for God's will;
The mountains, the valleys,
and the side roads sometimes taken,
Love for God I will always feel.
Thank you, Lord for allowing me not to miss
Such a beautiful life as this.

Notes/How This Applies:

Take The Next Step Ideas: Envision the life God has for you.

What struggle and/or shattered dream can you give to Jesus today?

Picture an area of your life being refined. Speak out loud this transformation!

Chapter 8

Daddy's Girl, Footsteps, and a Pen

This chapter includes a few of the poems my dad wrote throughout his years. When I was young, my favorite time of the day was 6 p.m.! 6:00 p.m. was when my dad would be home from work. Each day, I would hide behind the wooden, heavy front door I was barely able to move, waiting for his arrival home.

As my dad would enter our home, I would step behind him quietly like a mouse, putting my footsteps in his footsteps. Each day, the same scenario would take place at the entrance of our home.

After following his footsteps for a while, I would proclaim "It's me, Dad! Welcome home!!" My dad would act so surprised and happy to see me! Day after day, he would act as though this was the highlight of his day. Knowing he must be tired after working all day, he always had time to replay the same predictable scene of this dad and daughter welcome home scene!

My dad was deeply encouraged by seeing my husband Moe's journey with cancer. After seeing how much hospice meant to us during my husband's cancer journey, my dad felt God calling him to volunteer at a hospice in the county he lived in. My dad, in his eighties, attended the volunteer hospice training and became a hospice volunteer. I guess it goes to show us no matter our age, if we are willing vessels, ready to show God's love to others, God will open a place for us!

My dad shared many of his poems with hospice clients as the opportunity arose.

My dad loved attending church where he faithfully served as a Sunday School teacher for over forty years. Often, Dad shared his poems while teaching. My dad loved to speak of not missing God moments and how much he loved the Trinity: Father, Son, and Holy Spirit.

My dad received his Welcome Home into heaven at the age of eighty-four on Sunday, October 27, 2019 at 12:03 p.m.

We did not miss that God called him to his eternal home on a Sunday at 12:03 p.m.!! My brother, with tears flowing, whispered lovingly that Dad would have been leaving church at noon to go out onto God's mission field. And look at the minutes! 03, the Trinity! This was a God moment for sure!

I have always been a daddy's girl, and Dad and I had many daddy/daughter dates, which I treasure. Tears ran down my cheek like a river, wondering how I would handle missing my dad.

Now, in addition to grieving my husband, I am grieving my dad. I was still practicing being new at this grief journey. I felt, most days, I was a student who was failing in Grief 101!

It surprised me that I did not fall back into the learned reactions of hiding from my feelings. I was calm, as if to know Jesus was with me. Jesus cares for me, Jesus carries me. I have seen this firsthand. I knew to not linger in taking hold of the hand of Jesus. I finally did not run to that cleft that had my name engraved. I was hoping that cleft had turned into an open sunny field brightly glowing! I had learned to run only to the arms of Jesus, my Savior, my comforter.

I felt I must be denying my dad's death! I thought, "It must just be too much for me to bear, so I am not facing more grief." I then recognized I was analyzing where I was in my grief journey for my dad as well as for my husband. I quickly allowed myself to stop trying to figure it all out and just be me, right where I am, and as I am.

I truly believe the past losses I had been through helped me know God is good no matter what the circumstances , God's goodness is constant and God never leaves us.

I know I need my Savior each and every moment. Feeling God's peace that passes all understanding, I was reassured. It is reassuring to know even though I fail every day, I know God's grace.

In my dad's poems, I find truth, hope, and comfort, and I hope you do as well.

My dad inherited his mother's gift of writing poetry. My grandma, my dad's mom, wrote poems as well. The family loved sitting at her feet during our family reunions in West Virginia, my dad's birthplace, listening to her recite poetry from memory, not missing a word.

My dad wrote many poems throughout his life that we treasure. One of my dad's favorite poems he wrote is titled *God's Master Key*. As you read some of my dad's poems, you may sense him prayerfully whispering on the wings of a prayer for you, "Follow Jesus, the key, who unlocks peace and joy. Take a hold of God's master key. Turn towards God and accept the gift of love given by Jesus. Always cherish God's Master Key, designed for You and Me."

Inspirations, Scriptures, and Some of My Dad's Poems

Footprints

"From my first wobbly steps
Held by Mother's hand
To steps guided by Jesus
Marching to the Savior's Band.

Footprints on the way to Heaven
Oh what glory that will be
Thanks Heavenly Father, for
Footprints that I may see"[52]

Proverbs 3:1-5 (ESV) "My son, do not forget my teaching, but let your heart keep my commandments, for length of days and years of life and peace, they will add to you. Let not steadfast love and faithfulness forsake you; bind them around your neck; write them on the tablet of your heart. So you will find favor and good success in the sight of God and man. Trust in the Lord with all your heart, and do not lean on your own understanding."[53]

---

52 See footnotes.
53 ESV, See footnotes.

Heaven Bound

(by Wilson Milleson, my Dad)

"Living a life that is heaven bound
Is a life where true peace and joy is found.
Living for others is a victory for eternity.

It's a glorious victory of a heaven Christians will see.
We get there by repenting and living a righteous life today,
And maintaining a loving relationship with God's way.

Joining God in His Kingdom above
Is living in a place of eternal love.
It's a place where no tears are found.
It's a place based on love, peace and solid ground.

By living a life that's born anew,
We live in a spiritual life that is true.
So as we are born again in a spiritual way,
We are building a life that will not sway.

We are accepting a life of faith that is true,
And eventually we will see all in full glory too.
So let's give thanks for God's gift to His way
As we join friends in God's Kingdom today."[54]

---

54 See footnotes.

Faith

(by Wilson Milleson)

"Faith is to believe what we do not see
And, the substance of things we hope to be.
Jesus said a little faith is enough to move a mountain
Which will provide water from God's glorious fountain.
Christian faith is the process of investing trust and loyalty
In the Kingdom of God for eternal royalty.
When Jesus felt the touch from a woman's soul,
He said your faith has made you whole.
So, let's put our faith in God's way
And experience God's love and Kingdom today."[55]

Hope and Love

(by Wilson Milleson)

"Our hope and Heaven above
Is one of faith and love.
We cannot get there on our fame
But wholly lean on Jesus' name.
From doubt to faith, love and hope,
The Holy Spirit helps keep us in scope.
Have hope in the coming of God's Kingdom today,
As we enjoy serving others on our way.
Have hope in the promise of redemption now

---

55 See footnotes.

As we obey God's word and humbly bow.
Have hope in eternal peace in heaven, too
Assured that Jesus prepared a place for you."[56]

God's Compassion

(by Wilson Milleson)

"'God created each of us in His image of love,
And His love is always available for Heaven above,
When Jesus touched the leper and caused him to heal,
He asked him to be silent and not reveal.
The people were amazed at Jesus power to heal;
And, finally realized it was God's will that we feel.
When we suffer from hurts and ills,
God is compassionate and heals as He wills.
God is love, so expressing love is caring.
God is peace, so promoting peace is sharing.
God is compassionate and suffers with us,
And gives of himself through His son Jesus.
God forgives, so forgiving is the Godly way,
That allows us to walk close to Him today."[57]

---

56 See footnotes.
57 See footnotes.

Heaven's Gate

(by Wilson Milleson)

"Can you imagine entering Heaven's gate
Where there's no thought of the calendar date?
Where continuous love can be found,
And walking in the spirit is all around.
Where our Father, Son and Holy Spirit provides
The joy, peace and happiness that abides."[58]

There's Room in My Heart

(by Wilson Milleson)

There's room in my heart for God's wisdom and love,
That descends on us from The Holy Spirit's Dove.
There's room in my heart for Jesus caring attitude
That helps me live for others with grace and gratitude.

There's room in my heart for the Holy Spirit's comfort and care
That helps me hear the needs of others to share.
There's room in my heart for Jesus to light the way
So that my light can shine to others each day

There's room in my heart for God to guide me heavenbound
Which leads me to guide others to where peace is found.
There's room in my heart to have Jesus as my Savior
Which leads to the joy and peace of eternal flavor.

---

58 See footnotes.

So keep our hearts full of your abundant treasures
So that there is no room for world pleasures.
Thanks Heavenly Father for the gifts and blessings you share
Which leads to a home in your kingdom of eternal care.[59]

God's Master Key

(by Wilson Edward Milleson)

From nothing to creation,
From darkness to light,
From water to living creatures,
From God's image,
Man was created right.

> God's Master Key, freely given for you and me,
> Opens our way to Heaven's Eternity.

From Bethlehem to Calvary,
Jesus shows the way.
From death to resurrection,
He arose to a new day.
From the cross
Jesus did bear,
To the beautiful Heaven,
We all can share.

> God's Master key, freely given for you and me,
> Opens our way to Heaven's Eternity.

---

59 See footnotes.

From doubt to faith,
Love and hope,
The Holy Spirit helps keep us in scope.
From lost to found, turmoil to peace,
Our prayers will help us to release.
From life's journey to the other side
The Bible, a road map will provide.

> God's Master Key freely given for you and me,
> Opens our way to Heaven's Eternity.

From Mother's loving arms to abiding in the Master's love,
From Father's prayers to seeing the heavenly dove.
From families sharing and loving way,
To experience God's kingdom today.

> God's Master key freely given for you and me,
> Opens our way to Heaven's Eternity.[60]

---

60 See footnotes.

Notes/How This Applies:

Take The Next Step Ideas: Write a thank you note to someone who has influenced you or been there for you.

Think of someone who needs reminding that they are sealed and shaped in God's love. Consider calling them or writing them a handwritten note.

Thank you so much for your time reading my first book. When I was standing on that beach shore on Valentine's weekend 2017, unbeknownst to me, that would be my last trip to the beach with my husband.

God inspired the title of this book and the years of journaling in the hope to offer encouragement to others during their mountaintops and their valleys. This book has mainly focused on the journey of grief. We all can experience seasons of grief. It may be dreams that were shattered or the grief of any kind of loss or hurt. I pray you can lean into Jesus and know he walks alongside you. You are never alone.

My roads have taken me through hope, hurts, faith, fear, divorce, trust, mistrust, belief, doubt, miscarriage, dreams, births, adoptions, a second marriage filled with love, cancer journey, deaths, ministry, lies, plans for a future, eating disorder, depression, believing I am a daughter of the King, low self-esteem, and the restoration through a definition of me by being sealed in God's love and a growing personal relationship with Jesus that is here for us all.

Notice my journey waivers. I would like to say I checked off the box of fear and moved on, or I checked off the box of low self-esteem and moved on. Truth is I still waiver at times. I do best when I stay in contact with Jesus and stay in God's word. I take the next right step when I remove the mask of pretending and reveal the real me just as I am to God and also to someone I trust.

As a kite flying over the ocean, sometimes I am close to the sky and other times I fall. However, my Savior is there to catch me or to soar alongside me. I need my Savior each and every day, every breath along the way. Each day is a constant reminder of my dependence on God's love and grace. Know that you are being prayed for and you are dearly known and loved by God, your creator!

God bless you, and may you forever feel God's heartbeat in your hand. And when God gives you the gift of the dawning of a new day, fully glowing with His new sunrise and filled with His unchanging love, stop and give thanks. Remember, even if you discover the pieces of the pain of a shattered dream, your creator loves you and is always with you. Hold on to HOPE, and every chance you are given, delight in and dance right along with the birds celebrating God's gift of each new glorious sunrise.

Love, Debra

Notes:

Take The Next Step Idea:
Write your next step and go live as a beloved child of God, sealed in His love, shaped by His hand (He knit you together wonderfully). God sends you out to care for yourself and others.

You are sealed, shaped, and sent.

61

And The Birds Danced ...

Acknowledgements

To the memory of my dad, Wilson Edward Milleson, who taught me to not miss all the God moments around me. What a gift to have a dad who loved and served God: Father, Son, and Holy Spirit faithfully. He often reminded me that we get to experience heaven here on earth!! All along his journey, my dad lovingly portrayed the gifts of the fruit of the spirit with his faithful service to others.

Thank you to my mom, my first best friend. Thank you for always encouraging me.

Thank you to Carpenter's Son Publishing. Without them, I would not have been able to share my story. Thank you especially to Shane Crabtree, who has taught me so much about publishing, and was amazing to work with. Thank you to David Brown for doing such a great job editing. Thank you to Suzanne Lawing for her beautiful cover and layout. Thank you to the entire team at Carpenter's Son Publishing. You all do an incredible job ! Because of your dedication , my dream of sharing God's hope with others is a reality.

Referenced Footnotes

1 Zechariah 9:12, NIV, Bible Hub, accessed March 28, 2021. https://biblehub.com/niv/zechariah/9-12.htm.

2 Psalm 71:20, NIV, Bible Hub, accessed March 27, 2021. https://biblehub.com/niv/psalm/20.htm.

3 John 4:4-30, NIV, Women's Devotional Bible, Zondervan Publishing House.

4 Psalm 59:16, NIV, Bible Hub, accessed March 26, 2021. https://biblehub.com/niv/psalm/59.htm.

5 Psalm 139, The Message, Bible Gateway, accessed March 28, 2021. www.biblegateway.com.

6 Psalm 94:18, NIV, Bible Hub, accessed March 27, 2021. https://biblehub.com/niv/psalm/94.htm.

7 Psalm 94:19, NIV, Women's Devotional Bible, Zondervan Publishing House.

8 Colossians 1:17, NIV, Bible Hub, accessed March 27, 2021. https://biblehub.com/niv/colossians/1:17.htm.

9 Janet Eggleston, *It's In The Valley I Grow,* accessed April 5, 2021, https://www.allworship.com.

10 Smedes, Lewis, www.goodreads.com website , accessed April 6, 2021.

11 Merriam-Webster Online, "Hope"(n.d), accessed March 19, 2021, https://www.merriam-webster.com/dictionary/hop.

12 Romans 7:15, NIV, Women's Devotional Journal, Zondervan Publishing House.

13 https://www.wikipedia.org, "Grace" definition, accessed April 6, 2021.

14 https://ofhsoupkitchen.org, "Mercy" definition, accessed April 6, 2021.

15 www.lexico.com, "Balance" definition, accessed March 19, 2021.

16 Deuteronomy 31:6, NIV, Women's Devotional Journal, Zondervan Publishing House.

17 Jeremiah 29:11-14 , NIV, Bible Hub, accessed March 19, 2021, https://biblehub.com/niv/jeremiah/29:11-14.htm.

18 Isaiah 41:13, NIV, Bible Hub, accessed March 20, 2021, https://biblehub.com/niv/isaiah/41:13.htm.

19 Proverbs 11:1, KJV, Bible Hub, accessed March 19, 2021, https://biblehub.com/niv/proverbs/11:1.htm.

20 Matthew 6:33-34, NIV, Bible Hub, accessed March 19, 2021, https://biblehub.com/niv/matthew/33-34.htm.

21 2 Corinthians 4:7, NLT, Bible Hub, accessed March 28, 2021, https://biblehub.com.

22 Evans, Dale from book *Angel Unaware,* https://www.goodreads.com, accessed February 17, 2020.

23 Isaiah 40:31, KJV, www.biblegateway.com, accessed March 28, 2021.

24 Lewis, C.S., https://www.goodreads.com, accessed March 28, 2021.

25 Moody, Dwight, https://www.goodreads.com, accessed February 20, 2021.

26 Proverbs 4:25-26, NIV, Bible Gateway, accessed March 28, 2021, https://www.biblegateway.com.

27 Proverbs 3:5, NIV, Bible Gateway, accessed March 19, 2021, https://www.biblegateway.com.

28 Psalm 62:8, NIV, Bible Gateway, accessed March 20, 2021. https://www.biblegateway.com.

29 Merriam-Webster Online, "Trust" (n.d), accessed April 29, 2021, https://merriam-webster.com/dictionary/trust.

30 Mother Teresa of Calcutta, https://www.goodreads.com, accessed March 19, 2021.

31 Genesis 18:27, NLT, Bible Hub, accessed March 28, 2021, https://biblehub.com/genesis/18.

32 1 Timothy 2:8, NIV, Bible Hub, accessed March 19, 2021, https://biblehub.com/1timothy/2.

33 Eldredge, John, *The Ransomed Heart*, www.goodreads.com, accessed March 20, 2021.

34 Psalm 27:13-14, NIV, Bible Hub, accessed March 20, 2021, https://biblehub.com.

35 Psalm 5:3, NIV, Bible Hub, accessed March 28, 2021, https:biblehub.com.

36 Psalm 5:3, KJV, Bible Gateway, accessed March 19, 2021, www.biblegateway.com.

37 Psalm 3:3, NLT, Bible Gateway, accessed March 18, 2021, www.biblegateway.com.

38 Thoreau, Henry David, https://www.goodreads.com, accessed March 2, 2021.

39 Isaiah 43:2, NIV, Bible Gateway, accessed January 28, 2021, www.biblegateway.com.

40 Habakkuk 3:19, NIV, Bible Gateway, accessed March 21, 2021, www.biblegateway.com.

41 Braestrup, Kate, from book *Here If You Need Me*, https://www.goodreads.com, accessed March 19, 2021.

42 Clark-Coates, Zoe, www.allgreatquotes.com, accessed April 6, 2021.

43 Willard, Dallas, A Place Of Truth, www.goodreads.com, accessed April 6, 2021.

44 Psalm 94:18-19, NIV, Women's Devotional Bible, Zondervan Publishing House.

45 Philippians 3:12-16, NIV, Women's Devotional Journal, Zondervan Publishing House.

46 John 15:5, NIV, Women's Devotional Journal, Zondervan Publishing House.

47 Romans 15:13, NIV, Bible Gateway, accessed March 19, 2021, www.biblegateway.com.

48 Daniel 11:35, NIV, Bible Gateway, accessed April 9, 2021, www.biblegateway.com.

49 Camp, Melissa, from the movie *I Still Believe,* watched March 27, 2021.

50 Eldredge, John and Stasi, from the book *Captivating,* www.goodreads.com, accessed March 19, 2016.

51 Revelation 21:4, NIV, Bible Gateway, accessed March 28, 2021, www. biblegateway.com.

52 Personal Collection of Poems Written by Wilson Edward Milleson.

53 Proverbs 3 : 1-5, ESV, Bible Hub , Accessed March 28, 2021. www.biblehub.com

54 Personal Collection of Poems Written by Wilson Edward Milleson.

55 Personal Collection of Poems Written by Wilson Edward Milleson.

56 Personal Collection of Poems Written by Wilson Edward Milleson.

57 Personal Collection of Poems Written by Wilson Edward Milleson.

58 Personal Collection of Poems Written by Wilson Edward Milleson.

59 Personal Collection of Poems Written by Wilson Edward Milleson.

60 Personal Collection of Poems Written by Wilson Edward Milleson.

61 Picture taken by my daughter Abbey with her permission to share.

About the Author

Debra was born in Cumberland, Maryland, and moved to Lexington, North Carolina, at the age of seven with her family. After graduating high school, she attended and graduated from Presbyterian Hospital School of Nursing in Charlotte, North Carolina. Debra enjoys her career as a registered nurse with thirty-four years devoted mostly to the area of women's health through the field of public health nursing.

One of Debra's greatest joys is being a mom to her son, Jonathan(daughter in law Jessie), and two daughters Elizabeth(son in law Matt) and Abbey.

Debra has traveled the road of international adoption with the adoption of her daughters.

She enjoys spending time with her family and two dogs Cooper Jase (golden retriever) and Callie Grace (corgi), and makes her home in North Carolina.

Her hobbies include collecting and repurposing antiques, journaling, cooking, gardening, reading, spending time in the country and volunteering with a local golden retriever rescue group.

Debra enjoys sharing her testimony of God's story. She is an active member of her church in Winston-Salem, North Carolina, where she has been given many opportunities to grow in her relationship with Jesus. Debra has volunteered in the jail ministry, Celebrate Recovery, and The Landing. She facilitated a women's group for post-traumatic stress. She has participated in local mission opportunities and enjoys participating in and beginning new Bible studies.

Debra began and led a twelve-week class called, "Hope for the Hurting." "Hope for the Hurting" class participants expressed they experienced growing an awareness of feeling better prepared to walk alongside others with the unconditional love of Jesus after attending the class.

Debra has been a journal writer for over thirty years, and enjoys looking back at journal entries and seeing the wonderment and hand of God.

Debra's greatest desire for you is that your relationship with Jesus grows and you value each individual page of each chapter of your life and you know how much you are treasured and loved by God!

May you all enjoy God moments and the wonderment of God's love for us all! And, as you see birds in flight , slow down and envision the birds dancing with the amazing backdrop of a new sunrise glowing in your own journey of hope.